How Can I Grow As a Christian?

HOW CAN I GROW AS A CHRISTIAN?

A. STUART ARNOLD

BROADMAN PRESS
Nashville, Tennessee

Library of Congress Catalog Card Number: 74–178054
Dewey Decimal Classification: 248.4
Printed in the United States of America

TO
MY MOTHER
who has never thought to count
what she has freely sacrificed
for her Lord

CONTENTS

PART

5

How Can I Grow Through Personal Evangelism?

PART

6

An Encouragement

PART

I

The Challenge to Grow

The Need for Growth

The greatest change that can take place in the life of a man is spiritual conversion. In that act values are raised, new ambitions inspired, and latent powers are set to work. It is an act which separates the old life from the new in such a deep way that Jesus described it as rebirth and Paul saw it as death to the old and resurrection to newness of life in Christ. Everything is made new in that climactic experience. When it happens, the transformation is so significant that the convert may feel that he has reached the ultimate achievement. Old habits are broken, some friends are left behind, former attitudes are challenged, basic desires are changed, morals are improved, past sins are forgiven, and all things are made new. It is easy to conclude that nothing more is needed. That impression is often strengthened, particularly in the stronger evangelical churches, by the insistence upon the fact that we are saved by faith and not by works. We teach that salvation is a gift offered without cost and that our salvation does not depend upon our holiness but on the sufficiency of Jesus' atoning work. All of these things are true, but when they are totaled they often leave the impression that nothing more than that first decision is expected of the man who becomes a Christian.

This is very far from the truth, for the New Testament rightly asserts the fact that while conversion marks the end of the old life it is the beginning of a new one of unlimited opportunities for growth and progress. The new desires, values, standards, powers, relationships are given for our use as we grow in grace and in the knowledge of the Lord Jesus Christ. Surely one of the saddest passages in the New Testament is that where the apostle Paul is speaking with regret about the fact that he could not feed the strong meat of the gospel to the Christians of Corinth (1 Cor. 3). Their church was well-established, and they had had enough time to form party factions and fall out with one another. But they were still babes in Christ. Paul had to feed them with the milk diet of babies, because they were not able to take anything stronger. They had not matured. Paul points out that the deficiency was not his for he could have introduced them to deeper truths. It was they who did not have the spiritual equipment to make understanding possible; therefore, he had to give them an easy light diet. They ought to have grown in their ability to understand, and they should have matured in the faith.

So it is with many of us. We have failed to appreciate the fact that there is so much room for growth into the likeness of the Lord Jesus Christ that there never does come a time when we no longer need to grow. This lesson needs to be made plain to the new convert so that from the beginning of his new life he will realize that he has not arrived; he has only just begun. It is a lesson which the older Christian needs to hear so that he may continue to put effort into his discipleship. Without this emphasis, the Christian walk may soon become dull and uninteresting. When this challenge is faced, a fresh eagerness is retained even up to the end of the Christian's earthly life. There is always some new revelation to be grasped and understood. There is always some new demanding experience to be faced in the light and power of his grace. There is always some new service to be rendered in his name. He who stops growing stops being thrilled by the gospel news and he becomes ineffective in the work of the kingdom. Notice how eagerly the child learns new skills and rejoices in new experiences. This eagerness is a sign of youth. The eagerness of youth can be added to the strength of maturity in the life of the Christian who is aware of the fact that the Lord has so many wonderful things in his treasury that we need eternity to explore them.

We do not have to give close examination to the life of the average church to see the signs of immaturity. Many a deacon still prays the prayer that he learned as a boy. Many a congregation "switches off" the preacher who tries to explain even a simple theological truth. Blind prejudice about so many things reveals that lack of confidence that comes with maturity. Jealousies and bad spirit between members show that they are still children who have not learned to appreciate one another. (Compare 1 Cor. 1:11ff and 1 Cor. 3:1–4). Boredom with the gospel shows that the member has settled down in one place where spiritual comfort is preparing for spiritual sleep. Sincere vows are forgotten. Instead of leading to deeper faith, adversity destroys the little that was possessed. A refusal to make a full commitment is often shown in the person who clings to some old sin and hobbles along with one foot in the gutter. False pride leads a man to say, "I'm not one to push myself forward," when in honesty he ought to say, "I'm afraid to do that job in case my lack of growth and my spiritual poverty is shown up in it." Being hurt when someone, particularly the pastor, forgets to mention a name when he is trying to thank a long list of people is a too common evidence of immaturity. Anyone who has ever worked in any church will recognize in these, and many more such signs, lack of growth in the members of the churches. He will see them in himself too.

This failure to grow is all the more surprising when the Christian is made aware of all the spiritual helps that the Lord has provided to support him in the victorious life. There are so many aids that the Christian has scarcely any excuse for failing to make progress spiritually. Some detailed study of these helps is given in the various chapters of this book, but it will be encouraging to list them before we begin a consideration of how we may put them to work in our daily living.

The Church and Its Fellowship

These helps which God provides may be divided into three major groupings. First, there are the helps that are derived from our membership of the local church. Here helpful teaching and training is offered by able, consecrated people. Even in the smallest church we have all the strength of the denomination surrounding the small fellowship. From its greater resources we may obtain that which the local church may be too small to provide. But even the smallest church can provide that loving fellowship which is perhaps the greatest inspiration to spiritual growth that the Christian knows. It has been well said that one loving heart sets another on fire, and that can happen in any size church where members are in love with the Lord and with each other. This local fellowship also provides opportunities of service, without which there is no growth. The Christian gospel is really learned and understood as it is practiced. Serving the Lord in the work of the church is sometimes despised in these days, and people talk about "church-busyness," as though all the effort expended was pointless. In the fellowship we find the encouragement of people who are eager to see us grow in Christ and, very frequently, we have the inspiration of seeing their progress, often in the face of difficulties greater than the ones we face.

Material Helps

The second group of helps is found in the *things* that God has provided. If we attempt to list them we shall start with a book, the Bible, which is the most valuable of all these material helps. In its pages we have God's word and can read about God's ways with men. It is an objective statement of what he has done and can do for us. It contains the truth which can become our standard of evaluation of many of the major issues that make up our lives. It carries an authority which sets it apart from all other books and makes its study an imperative with every believer.

In addition to this unique guide, we have a wealth of writings about the Bible. Some are written academically to increase our knowledge of the Bible, its place in history, and its relevance to today. Some are written from a devotional point of view so that the Bible may be for us a source of spiritual strength and understanding. Other books will show the social implications of the Bible, and yet others will explain its relevance to personal needs. And so we can widen the circle to include books written to explain every facet of the Christian religion, from books on prayer to books on Christian influence on science, from books written for the simplest Christian to those written for the most learned theologian.

When we widen our thought beyond books to list other ways God uses to communicate help to us, we find that the richness of his provision is almost limitless. The musician, from the earliest days of the church to the present, has been used by God to bring men nearer to him. The types of music have been so varied that they almost require a listing because the Lord helps in such different ways by different styles of music. Plainsong delicately sung will elevate some; a country music gospel song enthusiastically sung will lift others. The poet has written his songs and the painter has expressed himself in form and color. Both have been used as servants of God in strengthening the spiritual understanding of the people. Films, radio, television, all make their offerings to us.

But we cannot stop here, for if the arts have been used to praise God so also have the sciences. Today's wonderful world can minister to the understanding of the greatness of our God and of the astonishing wonder of his redemptive work. As we push back the curtains of space, we simply learn how much greater our God is than we ever knew before. When we probe the depths of the atom, we find there the same pattern that controls the planets. When we touch these unimaginable sources of power, we see his greatness revealed in the infinitely small. For the writers of the Bible God has always been the greatest ("Thy power and thy righteousness, O God, reach the high heavens" Ps. 71:19, RSV.) who has had complete control of the smallest details (Who provides the raven its prey, when its young ones cry to God, and wander about for lack of food? Job 38:41, RSV.). Today science has expanded our knowledge at both ends—the great and the small—and has consequently given us such a tremendous picture of God that even the noblest songs of David scarcely suffice to praise him as he deserves.

> O wide-embracing, wondrous Love,
>   We read thee in the sky above;
> We read thee in the earth below,
>   In seas that swell and streams that flow.
>
> We read thee in the flowers, the trees,
>   The freshness of the fragrant breeze,
> The song of birds upon the wing,
>   The joy of summer and of spring.
>   HORATIUS BONAR

Spiritual Aids

Added to all these helps there is a third category which, if we used it as we ought, would multiply the effect of all the helps that we have already surveyed. God has promised his own personal aid to the believer. The Christian faith insists that God is not a God who sits in the seventh heaven of bliss utterly unreachable by needy men. He is involved in the lives of individuals. He has the ability directly to intervene in the life of the man who is ready to accept his advice and help. The incarnation did not represent a change in the work of God. He is always Immanuel, God with us. The numerous ways in which he tries to reach us, person to person, are so varied that the attempt to list them will make the believer ashamed of the poverty of his discipleship. We will look at a few of those ways.

Jesus has promised his resurrection presence in the very life of the believer. "I can do all things through Christ which strengtheneth me." He has assured us that he will be with us until the end of the world: he is an abiding, not a departed, Savior. The Holy Spirit will lead us and give us words to speak, he will equip us with special gifts for service. He will teach us all things. He will bring us to a sense of conviction about what we have to do. He will fill our acts with divine power. He will precede us in a work of preparation and he will follow our efforts with his confirming power.

But this is not all, for there is that wonderful tool of prayer that God has placed into our hands. No man has ever yet used it to its full effect but those who have really trusted in it have discovered that when a man puts it to use God can work wonders through it. Believers in every age have discovered that man may have a fellowship with God that has a reality at least as real as fellowship between very close friends. Prayer gives direction, purpose and power to life and consequently conveys an assurance of ultimate values that is difficult to find elsewhere. It is a vehicle of God's power which can be sent anywhere, into places where the Christian cannot go, across miles over which the Christian cannot travel, accomplishing things beyond his own power. The only limits that prayer knows are the restrictions that man's own lack of faith puts on it.

And so the list may be continued. Daily experience of a faith that works results in greater assurance and growth. When we put our faith to the test of experience, we discover a new sense of wonder at its practicality and its potential for joy. We go the extra mile out of a sense of duty and then discover that we have happily and unknowingly traveled two extra. We love our neighbor and then discover that he is capable of amazing love and understanding. We pass through the valley of shadow in a bitter experience and then glory in the sweetness of fellowship with him who is acquainted with our sorrows and our griefs. Though it appears an unreasonable paradox, the truth is carried home to us in our experience that we do not really possess our life until we lose it in him.

Perhaps the very richness of God's provision for us makes us poor stewards of these many helps. The young child, with a reasonable expectation of several decades of days stretching out before him, wishes away the days between now and Christmas. He is so rich. The man whose doctors have pronounced a sentence of death will make much better use of the treasure he continues to enjoy. Because God makes us so rich we feel that we can postpone using the many powers he gives us. We do it at the beginning of the Christian walk. "Tomorrow, tomorrow, I will decide tomorrow." Thus we start and thus we continue. "Tomorrow I will pray more." "I'm enjoying the pastor's preaching. I will let my Bible study go for the time being." "I have experienced much grace as God's power has carried me through that temptation. I just want to sit back now and relax." "God doesn't expect us to do everything. Our preacher explained the other day that Jesus did not mean that we should be perfect, only that we should try to be as complete as we can." Yet, in spite of our rationalizing and our self-forgiving, we recognize that our need for help is so great. Even the apostle Paul, that servant of the Lord beyond compare, was compelled to mourn his own personal failures and to protest that of all sinners he was the chief. God's rich gifts are sufficient for our every need, but there never comes a time in a man's life when he is so free of the weight of sin that he does not need that surge of divine energy which will lift him out of evil's downward pull. Every means of grace needs to be recognized, understood and employed as effectively as possible if we are to grow in him.

Training in Using His Gifts

It is sometimes suggested that there is no need to study how to use the various gifts that God imparts. Some would assert, misunderstanding a New Testament phrase, that if we depend upon the Holy Spirit we have no need of any instruction for he will teach us all things (see 1 John 2:27). We gratefully recognize that the Spirit is the best instructor that the Christian may have. There is little we can do in fact, to foster our spiritual growth if the Holy Spirit's life-giving powers are not available to us. Nevertheless we still have to work with that Spirit towards understanding and growth. The Scriptures nowhere teach that passivity is a condition of the Spirit's coming. Indeed it shows, on the contrary, that he comes to those who do not stop exercising themselves in prayer (Acts 1:14 to 2:1ff), to those who are busy planning their Christian service (Acts 16:7ff), to those who seek after his gifts (1 Cor. 14:1f), to those who have some work to do (Eph. 4). Like all the other abilities with which man is endowed his spiritual gifts need to be developed by training and exercise. It is not unspiritual to suggest that we need to improve our way of praying nor is anything artificial suggested by discussing techniques of evangelism. We need to know how to use every gift and opportunity we have to the glory of God, for our own spiritual development and for the winning of people for Christ.

PART

2

How Can I Grow Through Bible Study?

2

Is Bible Study Important

A good working knowledge of the Bible is a tremendous help in gaining the victory in the Christian life. This book brings us right into God's presence because it is his inspired word. From it men of every generation have derived direction and comfort. It tells the story of his patient dealings with men and of his self-offering on Calvary. Here we find comfort in the songs of the psalmist and the testimony of the apostle. Our guide for the individual life as well as for the corporate life of the church is found in its pages. It has rightly been described as the Christian manna, because it provides the spiritual food necessary for each day.

The New Testament makes it plain that the Scriptures were constantly used by the early church even in the first century. The record of Jesus' life shows us a man who knew the law, the writings, and the prophets well. He regularly referred to the laws and traditions of the Old Testament and did so with respect. Even when his fuller revelation of the Father carried him beyond the law, his emphasis was, "Think not that I am come to destroy the law, or the prophets: I am not come to destroy but to fulfil" (Matt. 5:17).

Jesus obviously saw himself as the one to whom the Old Testament writings pointed. In his story about the owner of the vineyard whose servants were murdered and who finally sent his own son (Matt. 21:33–41) he puts himself at the end of the age, the fulfilment of prophecy. This is specifically seen in his use of the Scriptures in the Nazareth synagogue. His familiarity with them is demonstrated by his use of Isaiah's picture of the coming one (Luke 4:16–21; Isa. 61:1–2). The work of the prophet influenced his teaching about his own task for he described his mission in terms of Isaiah's prophetic picture of the Suffering Servant (e.g., Matt. 20:28). Daniel's picture of the "Son of man" was familiar to him. He adopted as his own this title, filling it with a deeper significance (Dan. 7:13; Mark 14:6lf). Several sayings of Jesus carry the expectation that his hearers would know the Scripture passages to which he referred. "And have ye not read this scripture . . . ?" (Mark 12:10). His life clearly shows that he knew, loved and trusted the writings of the Old Testament. In this he gives us an example which we should follow if we are to grow in grace. If the Lord Jesus Christ profitted from a knowledge of the book, it is reasonable to suggest that his disciples would too.

It is logical to surmise that the early members of the church were led to preserve a new collection of writings by their recognition of the value of written records. The writings of the New Testament, in all their variety and abundance, were composed and collected within a century of his death. Historic records, church and personal letters, apocalyptic visions, were written and gathered for the further building-up of the church. The fact that they were passed down in such a wonderful selection and in such completeness tells us how precious these writings had become to Christians who wanted to grow in spiritual stature and in the extent of their influence upon the world.

The writings themselves contain testimony to the importance that the early church attached to the Scriptures. Paul's advice to Timothy, "Study to show thyself approved unto God, a workman that needeth not to be ashamed, rightly dividing the word of truth" (2 Tim. 2:15), is just one well-known example of the encouragement which was being given to new converts in those days. God had spoken through prophet and priest and, in later days, through the Lord Jesus Christ and he had conserved this revelation in the Scriptures. Therefore it is "profitable for doctrine, for reproof, for correction, for instruction, in righteousness: that the man of God may be perfect, thoroughly furnished unto all good works" (2 Tim. 3:16–17).

Supplementing the testimony of the stories of the New Testament itself we have many ancient documents which give further evidence of the important role played in the primitive church by the Scriptures. They were written in the early decades of the church's history and contain a lot of material describing how the Christian church turned to the Scriptures for guidance and comfort. In about A.D. 150 Justin Martyr wrote his *Apology,* in which he defended Christianity against its critics in the days of persecution under Roman emperors. In answering the accusation that the church was a secret society plotting the overthrow of Rome, Justin describes what happens at their meetings. He writes, "And on the day which is called Sunday, there is an assembly in the same place of all who live in cities, or in country districts; and the records of the Apostles *(i.e. our Gospels)* or the writings of the Prophets, are read as long as we have time. Then the reader concludes, and the president verbally instructs and exhorts us to the emulation of these excellent things."

When the church had survived the Roman persecutions and had become adopted as the religion of the Empire, in the days of Constantine, the Bible proved its value as a means of self-criticism and life. The scholarship of Augustine, coming from that period, has influenced the thought of both Protestant and Roman Catholic wings of the church—and he was converted in the reading of a passage from Romans. Centuries later, Martin Luther challenged the corruption of Rome and brought the doctrine of salvation through faith alone into the forefront of subsequent Christian thinking. It was the reading of the Scripture, and particularly the Galatians epistle, that enlightened him. The founding fathers of this nation were driven from their native land, three hundred and fifty years ago, by the love of the Book and then they found in it a source of solace and comfort in early difficulties. John Wesley took the world as his parish for he longed to preach Christ to every man. Wherever Methodist societies sprang up, the Bible was at the center. The world's greatest missionary of modern times, William Carey of the Baptist Mission in Serampore, India, knew the Bible's value was so great that he learned thirty-four Indian languages, translated the whole Bible into six of them and the whole of the New Testament into a further twenty-three! And these are a few of the great ones. For every one of them there were hundreds and thousands of smaller men who made this book part of their lives, in prison cell, on mission field, in dedicated service at home, in the midst of hardship and loneliness. God gave it; people have proved it.

In days when faith has been tried by persecution and apathy, criticism and scorn, the Scriptures have continued to provide strength and inspiration to those who trusted them. This century is a century in which faith is being tried by hostility. The Christian who would grow and make his contribution to improving the story of our times will find in the Bible an enlightenment it has never failed to give at any stage in the church's story. In its pages he will find reserves of spiritual understanding and power which the Spirit will make available to him. Standing on the sure foundation of the Bible his faith will remain firm in the face of the destructive winds of criticism and opposition.

How Can I Understand What the Bible Is?

One reason why people stop reading their Bibles with any regularity is that they do not really understand the nature of the book. To do a good job the workman needs to know his tools. Many who would use the Scriptures for growth do not know how it was constructed nor how it can be set to work in the ordinary life. They are afraid of using the book in any down-to-earth way because it has always been surrounded by an aura of piety and reverence. The great respect that we have for the Word of God has led us to bind its pages in unusual and expensive covers. The black calf covers with the lapped edges, the gold leaf beautifully laid over red on the sides of the book, the silk headbands and endpapers have made it quite different from any ordinary book on our shelves. A preacher jokingly said that he was afraid to take the new Bible his children had given him for Christmas to church because it had red covers! We have been careful to show our respect by putting it in a place of honor in our rooms and by not marking its pages. All this has tended to make us feel that this is a holy book which should not be mixed with ordinary books. But the Bible is a real book. Its histories are exciting, its prophetic words are as revolutionary as any twentieth-century protester might desire. Its poems are certainly among the best in any language. Its honest pictures of man's evaluation of his own and other people's lives is as frank as any modern psychologist's. Its stories of great figures penetrate to that which is good in our polluted lives. Its letters are from real people to real people. It is a human book. But when that is said we have to correct the statement by saying that the book is a divine book, divinely inspired for man's enlightenment.

The Bible Inspired

The mystery of how the Spirit of God controlled and directed the minds of those who wrote the Scriptures cannot be explained. We do not doubt that in some way the Spirit personally intervened and ordered the thinking of men with a clarity and an authority which compels recognition as being divine. There are some things we can say about inspiration, however, which will help us in our understanding of what the Word of God would say to us.

The Bible was inspired of God. That work was done as he entered into the lives and experiences of the people who wrote. He did not use them as automatic writing machines: he spoke authentically through their deep experiences to the problems and longings of men. At one time there were a lot of "fortune-telling" machines in public places. The top part had a convex mirror, coils and flashing lights, and tubes in it. In the middle there was a pen, mounted at the writing angle. On the front of the machine were two handles which the "subject" grasped. He put his coin in and the pen started to move. It "wrote" in script the "fortune" under "control." Then it all stopped and a printed card giving the result dropped out of the machine. It had been printed many months before! That is *not* how God inspired those who composed the sacred writings. He did not obliterate all that they were so that he might use the mechanism of their hand and eye to write his word. In a much deeper and more remarkable way he entered into and guided the experiences through which they were passing. Often those experiences were soul-searching experiences filled with anguish for the individual or the nation. In his own wonderful way the Spirit of God came into the thinking and the feeling of the writer and showed him ultimate truths that had been hidden from men. Because the truths were forged in the heat of such real-life experience, they speak to the needs of men of every age.

To clarify this point we take two examples, one from the Old and the other from the New Testaments. The example from the Old Testament is an obvious choice, for the remarkable prophecy of Hosea is such a dramatic demonstration of the way in which God revealed his eternal love to man through the faithful love which a man experienced for an unfaithful wife. Hosea married a woman named Gomer whom he loved. Her love for him soon died and she began to encourage the attention of other men. She left Hosea and began to sell herself. The time finally came when her attractions had gone and she could find no man to take her. All through her degrading course Hosea had kept on loving her and when at the last she had no place to go he sought her out and brought her back to his home. This brief account does an injustice to the moving story of the appalling torments through which Hosea went as he faced her unfaithfulness and watched her downward course to utter degradation and worthlessness. And the amazing thing was that he could love her through it! And search her out at the end! And forgive and restore her!

Then comes that astounding, inspired, breakthrough of a fully authentic revelation. The Spirit says to Hosea, "This is how I feel about Israel! She is my unfaithful wife who rejects me, but I shall love her beyond the worst that she can do!" Hosea passes on to all men the wonderful message that prepared for the unbelievable revelation of love given to us in the sacrifice of the Lord Jesus Christ on Calvary, when "God commended his love toward us, in that, while we were yet sinners, Christ died for us" (Rom. 5:8). God loves us, sinful though we are, and he will never let us go beyond the reach of that love. This is the message, true, authentic, inspired, divine. It came as a man struggled, as the Spirit struggled within him, as out of bitter experience God brought the sweetest truth of all—his indestructible love for rebellious man. It was not a coincidence that the man chosen to proclaim it was a man who knew the pain of unrequited, rebellious love.

Our New Testament example will be the brief letter of Paul to Philemon. The letter is about Onesimus, a slave owned by Philemon. Apparently Onesimus ran away from Philemon and tried to get lost in the multitudes of slaves in the greatest city of his time, Rome. There the boy was taken, possibly by slaves who were trying to help him, to the imprisoned Paul. Paul discovered that he knew personally the slave's owner! The apostle talked with Onesimus and eventually led him to the Lord (Philem. 10). Finally Paul persuaded him to return voluntarily to his owner. This was an unheard of thing because when a slave was restored to his owner it usually meant severe punishment, maybe death as an "example," but branding at the least. To help the young slave go back, thereby restoring Philemon's property, Paul wrote this letter to commend him to his master. The letter is full of Paul's love for the slave and for his owner. It contains persuasions of many types: Paul pleads his love for Philemon, Philemon's love for Paul. He reminds Philemon of the spiritual debt he owed, he tells how changed the boy is, that now he is more than a slave having become a brother. He suggests that he has authority to demand Philemon to take the boy back but he does not press this, he appeals to his confidence in his friend. It is a letter dealing with a specific problem of human relations. But it tells us as much about the transforming power of the gospel as any other writing in the Bible. It is an inspired word that has strengthened belief in the power of the cross and in the significance of obedience to the will of the Lord. It is undoubtedly inspired and is rightly part of our Scriptures. It too was forged in the real life conditions of a world that was just as full of man's sin, on the one hand, and immense potential for good, on the other, as ours is.

It is important to underline the fact that this statement of the way in which the Bible is inspired is based directly on the Bible's own statements. Many of the writers of the books in the Bible tell us not only why but also how they wrote. They give a reasoned account of how they were led to write and how they planned and assembled their material. Luke's statements are the most descriptive and detailed. He tells us that he was impressed by the work of other writers whom he had studied. As he thought about his unconverted friend Theophilus, he felt that his friend's need could be met more adequately by another book. So Luke tells us, "It seemed good to me also, having followed all things closely for some time past, to write an orderly account for you, most excellent Theophilus, that you might know the truth" (Luke 1:3–4, RSV). Notice particularly the phrases, "It seemed good to us," "an orderly account" and "for you." These words mean that Luke's own thought was concentrated on the story and that through this open channel the Spirit's leadership flowed in revealing power. He wrote under an inspiration that demanded the fullest use of all his intellectual and spiritual faculties.

Paul's letters open his mind to us as we see in his own words the reason why he wrote. In preparing for his planned visit to Rome he writes, "For I long to see you . . . I want you to know, brethren, that I have often intended to come to you (but have thus far been prevented)" (Rom. 1:11,13, RSV). To his friends in Corinth he writes, "I appeal to you, brethren, . . . that all of you agree and that there be no dissensions among you . . . For it has been reported to me by Chloe's people that there is quarreling among you" (1 Cor. 1:10–11, RSV). The Galatians letter begins with an expression of astonishment at the foolishness of the Galatians, then tries to correct them and at the conclusion underlines the personal writing of the letter by Paul's own hand. "See with what large letters I am writing to you with my own hand" (Gal. 6:11, RSV). "I write this to you who believe in the name of the Son of God, that you may know that you have eternal life," are the words with which John sums up his purpose for writing his first letter (1 John 5:13, RSV). His second letter ends, "I have much to write to you, but I would rather not use paper and ink; I hope to come to you" (2 John v.12, RSV). Jude begins, "Being very eager to write to you

. . ." These are men writing from the experiences and decisions of men, dealing with the ordinary problems of the churches and expressing their own personal hopes and affections. But the Holy Spirit fills their dedicated thinking and through their loving and ready cooperation he gives them an understanding of the truth that comes down to illuminate our thinking and deciding and following.

A clear understanding about the inspiration of the Word will give the Bible reader greater enthusiasm for his reading and it will increase his perceptivity as he reads. There is nothing magical about the Bible. A man does not have to possess some mysterious formula or know some secret code before he can interpret its message. It is an open book which has collected a whole panorama of human experience and says, "God is in this story," or "God can use this type of experience," or "This is what God said to a man who lived a life just like yours," until it reaches the climax where it says, "God was in Christ, living as a man but bringing that ultimate love, the love of Calvary, to substitute his obedience for the sin of man." It began with God speaking to people. That is why it can speak to us. It is a real-life oriented book.

When this fact is properly understood the Bible student will soon discover a desire to know more about the background of the Bible. At first he will see the simple master-truths that will strike him as he begins to read. Then he will learn more about the conditions under which the books were written and deep understanding will come. The reader's experience will be enlarged and he will change. Additionally with passing days he will have different needs and, as he goes back to the Scriptures with them, they will show him truths that he has not seen before. This is part of the practical art of Bible study. An understanding of how God inspires is a tool for study that will help the Christian grow in his faith.

A question needs to be answered here. How do we know that writings are inspired with an authenticity that gives them the undoubted authority of Scripture? This question has been very prominent at various stages of church history and though there have been some differences of opinion a most impressive unanimity over the issue persuades us that the Holy Spirit inspired the preservers of the books as well as the writers! In a long process of testing and sifting, the Holy Spirit led the church to a consensus about which books were acceptable and which were not. There was general agreement very early in the history of the church, though the final decision was not made until the invention of printing made the reproduction of the Scriptures in vast quantities possible. A comparison of those writings which were rejected with those that were accepted shows the wisdom and the guidance which the early church received. The Spirit which prompted the writing led the church in sorting out the chaff from the wheat, the real thing from the merely human. The writings which were rejected included so-called gospels which told stories about Jesus that made him look more like a magician than one who loved the needy.

The letters rejected, some of which purported to come from apostolic hands, are full of words that were no more than pedestrian repeats of the sublime themes of the Pauline epistles. The received texts of the various writings show an astounding conformity in their rich variety. They "belong" together but when even an amateur begins to read one of the rejected pieces he is immediately aware of the different quality in the writing. Over the centuries the approved texts of both the Old and the New Testament have been put to the test both in the experiments of scholars and in the experience of life, and they have been shown reliable. Maybe some things in the rejected books were good but the accepted books had to be authentic and dependable in every word.

Types of Writing

Another understanding that will help the believer grow through the reading of the Bible is the recognition of the fact that the Bible is not one book but is a collection of books of many types. The Jews grouped the books of the Old Testament into three sections, the law, the writings and the prophets. This is a good beginning but even in the Old Testament further analysis is a help. Within the *writings* there are histories (e.g. Joshua, Kings, Chronicles), books of wise sayings (e.g. Proverbs, Ecclesiastes) and of poems (e.g. Psalms, Song of Solomon). Within the division of *prophetic writings* we must notice that in Ezekiel and Daniel there are lengthy important apocalyptic passages. ('Apocalyptic' writings described in symbolic language, events expected to happen at a later time, often at the 'end of the Age.')

In the New Testament we have the Gospels. They are histories of the events of Jesus' life but they themselves contain several different types of writing. In them we have parables, apocalyptic passages, sermonic teaching. Acts is also a history. It is followed by a collection of letters by various people, usually apostles. The last book in the Bible is the most highly developed apocalyptic writing in the Bible, the Revelation of John.

As we study these books and letters it is a real help to have some understanding of what style of writing the writer was employing. If we know the form of the writing we shall approach it differently. When we read different forms of writing, we employ different means of understanding. In the daily newspaper we do not read the Wall Street pages with the same mental equipment that we use when we read the sports pages. When we read the Gospels we shall, for instance, put the greatest weight upon the words of Jesus and we will use what we read there in our interpretation of everything else in both the Old and the New Testaments. When we read the parables, we shall not treat them as if they were allegories. A parable illustrates one truth with a story taken from life. An allegory illustrates several truths; each part of the story has a definable and constant significance and the story may be beyond what we would normally expect in life.

It is important to recognize the difference between history, prophecy, and apocalypse. History tells what has happened and how God was active in it. Prophecy is an analysis of cause and effect. "If you continue to behave thus the consequences will be this," is the thought form of the prophet. This usually led the prophet to strong understanding of truths which are applicable to this day, with its very different conditions which are still subject to the same moral laws of cause and effect. Because the prophets' moral assertions were true, we see the working out of their projections in our own life situation. The apocalyptic writer was very like the prophet, but he was concerned about the consequence rather than the cause. He also used formal symbols to describe that which has not been experienced in terms of what has. His pictures are symbolic representations of true understandings which they dramatically represent. The beauty and preciousness of the New Jerusalem, for example, is richly described in John's use of pictures of gems and gold being used in her structures.

It must be clearly stated here that an understanding of these different forms is not an indispensable requirement for an understanding of the Word. Many a simple believer has been blessed by his study of the Scriptures without having even the dimmest idea of the nature of the writings he read with such trust. We live, however, at a time when the whole atmosphere of life is under critical analysis, and the Bible is not treated any differently. Knowledge about its nature will help the Bible reader to get the help he needs from it and to have a more informed grasp of its truths. The more we know about it the more effectively can the Holy Spirit guide our understanding of it.

How Can I Understand What the Bible Says?

Our Aim in Bible Study

There are two possible goals for Bible study. The book may be studied as a piece of literature or as a living word of God to each believer in his own situation. The two methods are not, of course, mutually exclusive; each can contribute to the other. However, for most people a choice has to be made for they do not have the time to do all the study they would like to do.

Study of the Scriptures as literature treats the Bible as a record of history or as a series of interesting documents demonstrating an increasing knowledge of the revelation of God in Judaism and Christianity. Such a study surveys the facts and ideas with care and sets them alongside the historic events and the common philosophies and religions of their times. The actual construction of the books is analyzed and comparisons made between the various writings. Questions about authorship, date, reasons for the writing, the people addressed in them, and the way local conditions of writer and recipient affected the writing receive attention. Fascinating studies of the various literary forms bring new appreciation. For instance, the study of the Psalms as fine examples of Hebrew poetry is an interesting literary exercise.

This type of study is of great interest to the person who loves the Bible, but for growth in the Christian life another style of study is required. Anyone, believer or not, can study the Bible in this way just as any student of English can study the plays of Shakespeare. The English teacher will discuss their date, their questioned authorship, the sources of the stories, when they were presented, how they have been treated through the centuries, how the social conditions of Elizabethan England are reflected in them. The quality of the ancient documents of the Bible can certainly stand such study. The believer, though, will want something much deeper than an academic study of the ancient documents to meet his spiritual need in the testing experiences of life.

When a Christian opens his Bible, he believes that he is opening his mind and heart to the living word of God. He believes that God can speak to his immediate condition through the words of the Scripture. He will ask not, "What does the Bible say?" but "What does the Bible say to me today?" In this book are enshrined the truths of God's revelation in the lives of people of different social strata living in many different situations over many centuries. Supremely the Bible is the record of God's amazing self-revelation in Jesus Christ. He is the figure to whom the Old Testament points and he is the one whom the New Testament portrays. In him the truth about the whole of life is revealed. This truth does not change, for if it did it would not be true. Our understanding of it changes with changing times. Experience enables us to see more of what God is saying to us in its pages. This book is grounded in history but its truth springs to life with new meaning to the man who is ready to hear. It is this truth which feeds us and equips us for the day's demands. In promising the gift of the Holy Spirit, the Lord Jesus Christ assured his disciples that he would lead them into all truth and bring all things to their remembrance. The reading of the Scripture becomes richly satisfying when this promise is fulfilled in an inspired understanding of the word. We grow as Christians when we listen to what God is saying to us, in our own situation, through the Word of Truth.

A note of warning needs to be sounded here for the devout Christian who might say, "That's the sort of study I need! I don't need that academic stuff!" If we recognize the two types of Bible study and then keep them far apart from each other we shall lose so much. Whenever it is possible, we should seek to learn as much about the Bible, in every way, as we can. Background knowledge of the actual historical surroundings of the writing will help us interpret it for our own times. An overall knowledge of the Bible will help us put our own day into its context more satisfyingly. The point of the emphasis that is made is that spiritual growth only comes as we apply the Bible's message to our lives. That is what makes the study of the Bible an imperative for the Christian. "The teachings of the New Testament make it very clear that Christian knowledge is incomplete until it performs that which it knows." [1] Any knowledge that we may gain by a study of content and of the historic, cultural and geographic backgrounds of the Scriptures is a help to this end. But the Bible only lives as we ask, "What does this say to me today?"

Reading Regularly

If we are eager to derive the most from our study, we shall read the Bible regularly. Just as the body needs its daily regular supply of food so does our spiritual life. After an initial enthusiasm has subsided we shall need some discipline to establish the habit. Some aids to this will be discussed later in this chapter. However, once the habit has been established the reading of the Word will bring such enrichment that any day passed without it will seem the poorer. The standard set by many churches and Sunday Schools is that we should read the Bible every day, just as we take food every day. That manna, gathered in the wilderness, that was kept overnight to the second day became sour and full of worms. But when the Israelites ate of it daily it was sweet and tasted like honey. When the Christian takes the manna of the Word daily it is sweet to his taste and it builds him up to everlasting and abundant life.

It is important to stress, at this stage, the fact that we should read enough each day to make it worthwhile. Some schemes for daily Bible reading suggest a portion of only a verse or two of the

Scripture. This is not enough. It gives a fragmentary idea of the Bible, with the result that we never get a feeling of the great fundamentals of our faith. These little bits feed the soul no more adequately than "snacking" provides a balanced diet for the body. Odd verses will not reach the heart any more than an arrowhead can penetrate without the shaft. Like everything else in life we can only receive vital help from the reading of the Bible if we will invest some real effort and time in it.

This leads to another necessary practical emphasis. The practice has grown up of reading at night immediately before going to sleep. This has some good points, for it is certainly wise to fill one's mind with great thoughts just before going to sleep. For most people, though, this is not the best time of day because they are too tired by then. What they want to do is to go to sleep but they persist in reading, largely because of their resolution. There is the peril that the reading will become an almost meaningless superstitious practice under such conditions. Certainly the clear word of the Lord will not be heard with any intensity. It therefore follows that we should try to find a regular time of day for reading which will give us some undisturbed moments while our minds are alert. For the businessman this may mean rising a little earlier to read before he leaves for his work. Maybe the mother will find her best time comes when the children have left for school and before the cycle of her routine starts. Maybe the high school student should open his Bible before he begins his homework. A sound principle to apply is that the best possible time of the day should be offered to the Lord, when the mind is alert and the pressures of outside interference are at their lowest.

Should daily Bible study be shared with anyone else? There are times when it should. It is a great thing for a newly married couple to establish the practice. They have new challenges which they need to face together and united Bible reading can help them in this. Then there are times when a person may be passing through a spiritual desert and can be helped by sharing in the devotional time of someone else. A new Christian can be helped in the discipline of regular reading by a mature Christian who is prepared to share his Bible study with him. Family Bible study and prayer, planned to meet the needs of the youngest member, can unite a family and start a good practice among the children. The parents of families who do this will almost certainly find that they have to do some preparatory reading and thinking and praying if they are going to be able to help their little ones.

Apart from situations like these, it may be correct to make the general statement that individual Bible reading should be the rule. A man needs to be alone when he talks to God and listens to what he has to say. Even those nearest and dearest can divert our thinking away from what the Lord would say to us. Maybe the ideal would be for families to share a time of study together and then set a period of the available time aside for each one to use personally. This is an ideal that few could reach, so we realistically recommend that if a choice has to be made it is usually better to choose to read alone. If each individual in the family reads the same passages there might be an informal time of sharing of thoughts before the day is done, particularly when there has been something in the reading which has a pointed reference to the family's life.

How to Plan Daily Reading

Purely random reading of the Scripture is not to be recommended. It lacks that orderliness in which today's study builds on yesterday's and which tomorrow's advances thinking a further stage forward. This type of reading usually deprives us of the help of background knowledge of the passage studied. It also seems to assume that there is no reasonable development in the thought and teaching of the Bible and that is not the case!

There are many organizations which publish sets of daily Bible reading notes. These are often most helpful. They provide a systematic reading plan and, in the notes, often give us ideas that stimulate our own thinking. The thought in the notes should not, however, be allowed to take the place of our own thinking. Many denominational and interdenominational publishing houses print sets of daily helps. Their titles and availability can easily be discovered in the denominational press or from evangelical magazines.

Some denominations have well-developed Sunday School programs and their periodicals suggest daily readings which are chosen to support the passage being studied in the Sunday School hour. These are obviously tremendously helpful to the Christian because they enrich his experience in an area of thought that can be shared with his friends on Sunday. Some denominational daily Bible reading notes meet this need too.

Some people are dissatisfied with such notes because the passages set are too brief or do not systematically cover areas of the Bible. They need something which will help to avoid that fragmented knowledge of Bible stories which cannot relate Moses to Elijah or Ezekiel to Isaiah. For those who wish to cover the whole Bible the American Bible Society has a leaflet which shows how this may be done in one year through fifteen minutes of reading a day. The leaflet is entitled, *My Bible Reading Record*. The leaflet also separates the books of the Bible into the different types of literature. Many books written to help in Bible study suggest lists of passages that might be read in order to cover the main themes of the Bible in greater or lesser detail and time. Other lists suggest "favorite passages" or "key chapters."

Another very helpful way of studying the Bible, which will appeal to the student who really wants to dig deeply, is that of studying entire books. The fact that daily Bible reading notes often select their passages from chapters scattered in different parts of the Scriptures may be helpful in following themes, but they suffer the disadvantage of being piecemeal. The consistent study from verse to verse and from chapter to chapter of one book at a time can build the Christian's knowledge of the Bible. It can also have a greater impact on his living because the impression of the book builds up day by day. Those who wish to study in this way will need the help of an appropriate expository commentary. It is impossible in this place to recommend titles because needs and backgrounds vary and there are so many good ones for every book of the Bible. The student will be able to get advice from his pastor, from his church librarian, from assistants in the local book store, or even from the librarian in the local public library.

The commentary chosen should not be an academic one written for scholars but a more popular book that expounds the Scriptures. Most commentaries have two main sections. The first part is introductory and covers such matters as authorship, date, and the occasion for writing. Possibly, in this section, a review of the contents of the book and its distinctive themes may be discussed. The second part of the book will be the commentary itself, where the writer will discuss every part of the writing, moving on from verse to verse. Some commentaries use the text of the King James Version while an increasing number are based on the new modern translations. Care should be taken to see that the words of the commentary are not read more diligently than the words of the Scriptures. We should also try to secure some knowledge of the theological stance of the writer so that we may take this into account in our evaluation of the opinions he expresses. The commentary allows us to listen-in to some great Christian thinking about the passage but we need to think and meditate too if we would really grow in understanding.

Using Translations

There are some simple aids which can help us tune in to what the Spirit would say to us in the day's reading. The use of different translations is of great assistance in hearing the old words in a new way. We do not forget that a lot of people believe that the King James Version is beyond compare. There is no doubt that it is so superb a translation that the Holy Spirit must have controlled the minds of those who, nearly four hundred years ago, found those beautiful words and phrases to convey the divine word to successive generations. That version has enriched our theology and has shaped the civilizations of the west. The fact that whole passages are known by heart by many is a testimony to its quality and inspiration. The reading of new translations with the King James Version adds understanding when old thoughts are put into new words from today's vocabulary. The whole study is enriched. It is a good plan to read the passage first in a new translation. This can be done quickly with rapid comprehension because modern speech communicates more quickly than does the translation of 1611. Then turn to the King James Version to retain a familiarity with its distinctive riches and truths. If several new translations are owned they may be used to try to understand difficult points, but in one course of reading we should use only one modern translation. If more are used the study can become a literary exercise and we shall miss the message in the multiplicity of words.

There are three modern translations of the whole Bible available. The oldest of these is the Moffatt Bible which was translated forty years before the Revised Standard Version was completed. The latest complete version is the New English Bible, which was the work of an interdenominational team of British scholars. In the New Testament alone there are several other translations into modern speech. We will name only the Today's English Version because of its distinctive, yet restrained, use of modern speech in words and idioms. There are distinctive features in each of the other translations which lead readers to treasure one above the others as the richest in a veritable treasury of resources.

But How Can I Really Hear?

For those who are prepared to take the trouble there is a wonderful way of receiving help every time they read their Bible. This is a simple system but it requires some thought and a little writing. The idea is this. Towards the end of each day's study period the reader asks the question, "What is God saying to me in this passage?" After some contemplation, he then writes down in one sentence what the message is. This message may sum up the meaning of the whole passage or it may be prompted by one verse or phrase only. It may be that the actual reading itself brings to remembrance something else: the verse of a hymn, a thought in a sermon once heard, a book once read. It may be that the Bible passage will suggest some action that should be taken. It may challenge the reader to fuller commitment in some aspect of the Christian life.

This thought is to be written down in one sentence. If it is not written down the thought will remain nebulous and vague. Putting it into words, in writing, on paper seems to inscribe it on the memory too! This writing will also discipline thinking so that a "feeling" is reduced to one idea in one sentence. The thought is distilled into one sentence so that the mind can hold it and use it during the day. This practice clarifies thinking and enables us to retain and apply the thought. Without some device like this it is unlikely that our undisciplined minds will retain any word from the Lord. Undoubtedly it will train the mind to hear and the heart to respond. The record will also provide us with a spiritual diary which will show us the path we have trod. Often when we look back and read what we have written months previously we shall be surprised by the spiritual perception that we showed and so we shall be blessed a second time! Believers who have used this system have discovered that sometimes in the mature Christian life the technique is outgrown but then times of spiritual dearth come again when the heart is heavy and the ear is deaf. How helpful it is then to know how to use this method to regain one's nearness to the Lord and the peace and strength that follows. Growth is necessary all through life and we need to be constantly alert when the words we read are so familiar that they have lost their meaning. There is always some word from the Lord for the man who has trained himself to hear. The development of this skill in hearing has the promise that the Bible need never become dull and that the more we listen to it the more sensitive do we become to what it has to say to us.

It is impossible to exaggerate the importance of daily, devotional Bible reading for the Christian who would grow. When God's word is taken seriously, the believer's life comes under his direction more positively, it grows in strength because of the spiritual food it receives and it deepens in joy as assurance constantly comes from the inspired page.

NOTES

1. James D. Williams, *Guiding Adults* (Nashville: Convention Press, 1969), p. 14.

PART
3

How Can I Grow Through Prayer?

Is Prayer Important?

Most Christians would answer that question with a very definite, "Yes!" The church has always taught that prayer is essential to the development of the Christian life. But, if we face this question honestly, the behavior and practice of most churchgoers would tell us that they really believe that prayer is a help but is not essential for the full life. Days of national prayer, called by the political leaders, inspire us and we think that they are good. Times of climactic experience, like a wedding or a death in the family, will drive us to pray and we are grateful for the outlet it offers to our stirred spirits. Sometimes, when the lamp burns low and we take time to notice it, we try to brighten the flame with regular prayer. For a time it really does help and we wonder why we do not always take time for God, then things happen to divert us, our confidence rapidly gives birth to complacency and our prayer life slips away again into the nod of the head that we give to God each night or when we eat with Christians!

This may be something of a caricature but there is certainly enough truth in it to remind us that we do tend to spend more time in talking about prayer than in talking in prayer. Why is prayer important? Because it is the only means we have of discovering God's will for us and of securing spiritual resources with which to do it. Bible study makes its contribution by showing us how God acts and how men should respond. But it is in our own personal prayer life that the basic principles of the Scripture are made personal to us. That is where the Holy Spirit takes the general principles and applies them to the particulars of our life situation. We shall notice later in this chapter how our Lord himself constantly felt the need of prayer for the maintenance of his fellowship with the Father. If he needed it, we certainly do. Those who were with him saw this, and when they carried the responsibility of organizing and propagating the gospel forces in those first days after the crucifixion, they turned constantly to prayer. In Acts Luke lists the names of the twelve-less-one, and tells that "all these with one accord devoted themselves to prayer" (Acts 1:14, RSV). The story of Acts and the testimony of the Epistles is that these men found that prayer works. They were determined to use it as they faced the overwhelming odds that were stacked against them in the Roman Empire.

But we need not limit our thought to the days of the New Testament. Take the life story of any great servant of the Lord of any generation and you find a man of prayer. John Wesley is reported to have been so dependent upon prayer that in his long journeys across England on horseback he thought time for prayer was more important than time for sleep. He used to get up at three o'clock in the morning to have time to pray! William Carey, working in his shoemaker's shop in the English midlands, hung a map of the world on his wall. He prayed that God would stir up the church to send missionaries to distant "heathen" lands, and he was the first to go. The great nineteenth-century revival, in which Moody was a leading figure, began in a layman's prayer meeting in Chicago and spread eastwards largely through businessmen's prayer meetings. It leaped the Atlantic largely through laymen's prayer meetings to run through the length and breadth of Great Britain and then to cross to the European mainland. And not only have servants of the Lord in the church found that prayer is essential but men of every profession have discovered that prayer opens doors. It is thrilling to know that the first time a door was opened on the moon astronaut Bud Aldren prayed to the God of all the universes, while down on earth his home church prayed with him. The learned and the simple, the rich and the poor, the famous and the unknown, have found that God's ear is never deaf when they talk to him.

Prayer keeps the lines of communication open between the Father and his children. When we neglect it, it is as though we are telling the Father that we can get along without him very well. James Montgomery was much nearer to the truth of man's dependence upon the power of prayer when he wrote:

> Prayer is the Christian's vital breath,
> The Christian's native air.

It is essential for the health of the spiritual life because it is the atmosphere that suits us best, like the air of the place where we were born. In it we can thrive. God sometimes uses the person whose prayer life is weak to accomplish his great purposes but more often he uses that person whose readiness to respond is indicated by his willingness to listen. If we want to be used by him, we shall keep our ears attuned to his call. It we want to grow as Christians, we shall do well to put the practice of prayer foremost among our activities.

PART 3

Can Prayer Ability and Skill Be Developed?

Is it right for the Christian to practice prayer as though it were an art? Is there any need for a technique in prayer? Ought we to bring methods into a relationship of dependence like prayer? It is a commonly held view that a Christian should enjoy such a close relationship with his Lord that his prayer life will develop naturally without any conscious effort on his part. To introduce aids of any sort seems artificial to some and to others it may seem that such things do not belong to evangelical Christianity.

The example of our Lord's own disciples teaches us to think differently about this. His prayer life was beyond compare and they were aware of it. Men who were with him in those hectic months of his ministry felt that he had a close unbroken relationship with his Father. There was a power in his life that was more than human. Though he experienced our sorrows and knew that tiredness that comes to body and mind after a hard day's work he was able to renew himself. In the midst of all the demands and attacks which were made upon him he kept his composure. He had a deep inner peace because he retained by prayer his unity with the Father.

The Scriptures show his method for dealing with such times of exhaustion. He did not depend upon some peculiar, mystic relationship between himself as the incarnate God and the Father in heaven. Because he was identified with us, he used that means of renewal which is available for us too. He used to withdraw from the crowd into a place apart where he could spend the whole night in prayer with the Father. Whether it was in the midst of the clamoring crowd or in the loneliness of the night of betrayal, the Lord Jesus Christ gained strength in prayer. This accession of strength was so obvious that those nearest to him envied his ability, "Lord, teach us to pray!"

A significant aspect of this story is that Jesus immediately did what they asked, as though he had been hoping for such a request. He did not rebuke them nor did he suggest that instruction about prayer would not be helpful to them. Instead he gave an example prayer which was simple enough for a child to understand and profound enough to claim the contemplation of the saints of all ages.

Other stories reveal that Jesus himself took the initiative in discussing method in prayer. He commented on the practice of those who liked to pray in public and to use many words. He told stories about people who received an answer to their pleas because of their importunity. He compared the asking-prayer of petition to the Father with the child's request of his parent. Jesus even asserted that the gift of God's mighty powers could only be committed to those who had mastered the art of prayer through long practice, "Why could we not cast the demons out?" they asked. He answered by saying, "This kind goeth not out but by prayer and fasting" (Matt. 17:21).

Prayer is an art that can be cultivated. In its cultivation the believer comes nearer to his Lord. That is a desirable goal for any Christian who wants to grow. The privilege of coming into the presence of the Lord God is something that ought to be thought about deeply if the Christian is to make the fullest use of it. The instruction given to Moses is still meaningful. "Take thy shoes from off thy feet for the place whereon thou standest is holy ground." At the same time the coming needs to be as simple as the coming of the child who rushes to his father's side asking, "Daddy, may I?" Our God is at once transcendent—far above us in power and holiness—and immanent—knowing us more perfectly than we know ourselves and always at hand to aid with the smallest of our concerns. This distinctive paradox of the Christian faith, a God far above and at hand, was never approached even by the prophets of the Old Testament who seemed unable to lay aside their sense of separation from the awe-ful God whom they worshiped. When we forget either aspect of the nature of the God whom we worship, we make our prayer less rich than it might be and neglect a privilege which the most deeply spiritual men who lived in times before Christ never knew. "Father, thy name be hallowed" (Luke 11:2 NEB).

3

Order in Prayer

Real help is derived from order in prayer. Clear steps in orderly succession will help a Christian to reach forward to a richer, fuller life through more balanced prayer. Without it prayer can so easily become a self-centered asking for things. Prayer is much more than that! It is a listening as well as a talking experience. It is a time when a believer allows God to move into his life as well as being one where he deliberately brings his recognized needs and longings to God. Someone has said that we think prayer is asking God for what we want but it is asking God for what he wants.

Prayer needs to be outward-going because it is an approach to God. This is the *objective* aspect of prayer. In it the believer looks out from the smallness of his little world to glory in the matchless perfection, the unconquerable power and the indescribable love of God.

Prayer is also *subjective*. It should be an honest examination of failure in the light of Christ's life. The inward look will also take note of needs of all types and will seek to cover the needs of others too. Where objective prayer looks out from the believer to God, subjective prayer allows God to look into every part of his living to cleanse and renew, to help and to bless.

A satisfying balance between the objective and the subjective can be obtained by using a simple order which assures the inclusion of the main factors but does not limit the leading of the Holy Spirit. Some writers of books of devotional helps say that there should be seven elements in prayer: praise, thanksgiving, confession, repentance, intercession for others, petition for oneself, and adoration. The value of such a detailed list of steps may be easily seen. Each step takes us nearer to our God in worship, (the objective side) which inspires a desire for cleansing, which is so necessary before we bring our asking prayers, (the subjective side), which will issue again in praise. Such a list is ideal. But for most Christians it is too long and demanding. It is so demanding that the effort of reaching forward through it might well destroy the spontaneity and confidence which should run through all believing prayer. We need some structure to give shape and direction but not so much that it restricts the soul's response to the Lord as he comes to us in prayer. Four major elements are therefore drawn out of this list and they are set in the form of a simple mnemonic which can easily be recalled. The four elements are

> *P*raise
> *R*epent
> *A*sk
> *Y*ield

Praise

Whom do we approach in prayer? Ours is no household God that can be ordered around for our own selfish ends. He is no talisman that can be carried about in the pocket. He is the Lord God Almighty, the one God over all. Whenever we come into his presence we should be aware of the glory of the Lord of hosts and the equal wonder that he lets us enter into his presence. Every prayer should therefore begin with praise. His wonderful works in creation and redemption should fill our hearts with gladness and with song. Putting it theologically, we can praise him for his unbounded knowledge and wisdom, his invincible power and his presence in every place. Or we can praise him for the magnificence of the clouds piled high into the heavens against a shining blue sky, or for the gay laughter of children echoing through the woods on a winter day, or for the coolness and sweet odor of rain on the dust, or for the scent of the violet, or the silk of the cat's fur. We can praise him with the deep emotion that the music of a mighty organ evokes or with the peace which comes when our wrestling with him in prayer has brought submission to his will. We can praise him for the release of love and joy that results when we stand at Calvary and know, in part, the boundless love of his heart. We can praise him when we read his word that tells us more about him every time we open it. We can praise him when his Spirit moves in our hearts and teaches us so much about ourselves. Or when he moves in another's heart and we see a soul saved, a life changed. Where can we end our praising? What power and delight will come to us in our prayer—and in each part of our life as a by-product—if we let our imagination loose in praise instead of keeping the voice of praise stifled by our approved church forms and phrases. The prayer that begins with glad praise, wide and all-embracing, puts the wings of faith onto spiritual experience and sets our spirits free to glory in all that he has done and will do for us.

If the Christian resolves that he will begin each prayer with praise, a priceless by-product will result. Every corner of his life will be touched by the radiance of the Lord's presence. As he goes through life he will, at each step, look for some new cause for praising God. In every shifting scene he finds some new revelation of the presence and activity of God. Tomorrow he wants to praise God in some fresh way so today he looks for some distinctive activity which he will notice and remember. He becomes sensitive to God's activity in his world and life. This consciousness contributes to that spontaneous prayer that we shall discuss later in this chapter.

The praise of God involves the whole of man's being in prayer. God can be praised for himself or for his works. He can be praised for all that he did through the Lord Jesus Christ and for all that he continues to do through the work of the Holy Spirit. Our praise may center on our own experience or on what we learn from others.

It can be the formal approach of the worshiper who cries, "Holy, Holy, Holy," or the glad shout of the child of God who cries, "Wow . . . That's great!" The introduction of order into our prayer need not make it formal and dead; it can bring depth and a real satisfaction to what so easily can become self-centered and shallow.

Repent

But who has any right to intrude into the presence of God? David's great resounding statement reminds us of the centrality of repentance in our relationship with the Lord. "Who shall ascend into the hill of the Lord? . . . He that hath clean hands and a pure heart" (Ps. 24:3–4). It is a fact of human experience that a man only feels his need of repentance, with its consequent liberation of forgiveness, when he really comes into contact with God.

Almost all men become aware of the seriousness of their short-comings when they compare the holiness of God with their own failures. They see the poverty of their own attitudes when they have concentrated upon the abundance of his giving. Not only does such comparison make sin (and all our deficiencies) obvious to us but it defends us from the danger of rationalizing it all away as psychological quirks, or as sociological offenses, or as harmless human traits. Sin's real nature is seen clearly as rebellion against God. The prayer that begins with praise will help a man to that necessary act of renewal which is repentance combined with the forgiveness that follows it.

Let us try to see what repentance means daily in the continuing Christian life. In the transforming experience of conversion repentance is that act in which a person "changes his mind," as the derivation of the Greek word *(metanoia)* defines it. It is not a series of acts leading to righteousness. That is the process of sanctification. Repentance is that initial change of direction which is the vital *beginning* of salvation and sanctification. Yet there is a need for daily renewal of our restored relationship between the believer and the Lord. Every day we do things that cut us off from God, even though we are resolved that this shall not be so. Therefore every day we should feel an urgency to come to him in repentance, in which experience adds remorse to the original change of mind.

In this part of our praying honesty is a basic requirement. It is so easy to drop into that meaningless phrase with which we often end our prayers, ". . . and forgive us of our sins." The prayer of repentance needs to be more soul-searching. The offences against God's will need to be identified and owned so that we may rejoice in the forgiveness that our loving God grants. Perhaps this is one of the best ways of overcoming our faults and of destroying our bad habits. A daily evaluating, in the presence of the Lord, of our successes and failures will soon make us aware of the trends in our life. Changes in circumstances, contacts with new people, the influence of different ideas, lead to changes in our behavior which, in their turn, may lead to good or bad habits. Daily searching of one's life, laying it open before God, reveals trends before the bad ones have time to take hold!

Questions that help in a self-examination that will precede meaningful confession should include at least the following three. Have I hurt or helped other people today? Have I been true or false to myself today? Am I nearer to or further from my Lord as a result of this day's living? An honest appraisal based on questions similar to these, of our thoughts, words and deeds will add meaning and power to our living. Power comes because God always fulfils his promise, "If we confess our sins he is faithful and just to forgive us our sins and to cleanse us from all unrighteousness" (1 John 1:9).

Ask

This is that type of prayer that makes up most of the praying that people do. There is nothing wrong with the asking prayer. On the contrary, the Bible encourages it and urges us to place all our needs before our heavenly Father. We are to ask in faith, without doubt, and to go on praying until we have an answer. We are to bring serious matters to him because he is great enough to be able to deal with them. We are to bring small things to him because his greatness is seen in his care for the details of his world, the sparrow that falls and the flower that withers unseen.

In the asking part of our prayer we should think on two levels—the needs of others and our own needs. Great strength can come to the man whose love for people is expressed in intercessory prayer. Intercessory prayer is that prayer in which the Christian goes to God to ask for blessing for others. What a privilege it is to use prayer to help carry the sorrows of the bereaved, to cooperate with the doctor and nurse in the care of the sick, or to put a hand on a student's shoulder in the examination room, or to hold a shield of faith in front of a soldier in battle, or to uphold a friend as he flies in the skies. What extra joy is ours and hers when we are able to pray for the young bride on her wedding day, or a pastor as he begins a new ministry, or a couple as they move into a new house. Or to pray that our friend's success may not lead him into temptation. This procession of suggestions is not offered as a check list. It is an attempt to indicate that there is a multiplicity of things that we ought to think about when we remember others. Too often our prayers are so poor and limited in their range because we do not consecrate our imagination in prayer. Because we have a poverty-stricken approach to God, we simply do not see how rich he is!

Yet when we have listed all these things, we have not thought about the most important prayer that we can offer for others. That is the prayer for the salvation of individuals. We shall experience a real depth and urgency in prayer when we pray that the love and knowledge of the Lord Jesus Christ may come to persons who do not know him. It may not be wise for the wife to announce to her unsaved husband that she is going to pray for his conversion for that will very often produce a resistance to the Spirit's working which will be a hindrance to the work. Sometimes this is not the case. Many men would gratefully admit that they finally began to think about their relationship with the Lord because they knew that their mother was lovingly and persistently praying for their conversion. But, as a general rule, it is wiser to pray without telling the object of our prayer what we are doing!

Prayer for conversions seems to have a quality all its own. Because it is concerned about eternal matters of life and death it takes on an intensity not felt in even those prayers that we offer for physical healing. When we pray for the conversion of people whose lives have become tangled and snarled by their efforts to get the most out of life without Christ, our prayer becomes cross-centered. When a person's eternal salvation takes a vital, central place in our prayer, it is unlikely that we shall get lazy about it. Just as Jesus wept over man's sin so shall we, and this will bring us a little nearer to that urgency of prayer that he knew in Gethsemane.

When we have put others first, we may turn to our own petitions. There should be a confidence in approaching the Lord in prayer, even as we ask for blessing for ourselves. He is a God who gives generously (Jas.1:5). His powers know no limit. He knows how to give good gifts to his children. The Scriptures are unbelievably rich in their witness to God's readiness and ability to hear and answer prayer. We may claim for ourselves the assurance of Paul's statement, "[He] is able to do exceeding abundantly above all that we ask or think" (Eph. 3:20).

Should the "objects for prayer" that we bring for ourselves and others always be related to spiritual matters? The answer is suggested by the wealth of promises regarding prayer in the Scriptures. There is nothing in this world outside God's control. Therefore there is nothing in our experience beyond the range of prayer. Any concern may be presented to God. Material well-being, physical and mental health, problems and decisions, spiritual longings and shortcomings, are all part of prayer. Distance may be spanned when we remember people far away and the victories of tomorrow may be gained in the prayer of today. Time and space are no barrier to him, and we can touch the lives of people whom we have never seen and we can use prayer to prepare for unknown challenges that lie in the future. Nothing that concerns his children is too small for the Father's interest nor anything too big to be beyond his power to accomplish.

Yield

When we ask our friend to do a favor for us we always thank him for having listened. So in our prayer it is good, before we finish, to turn our thoughts away from our own desires and petitions to look into the face of the Father with whom we have been talking. He is a great and mighty God, holy and full of grace: he also knows us through and through and yet loves us. Our offering of thanks to him will lead us to offer ourselves too, not in repayment but in outgoing gratitude. If we identify this God as the one whom we approach through the mediation of the Lord Jesus Christ, who purchased our way back to God, our surrender will be more complete.

The wonder is not that he is able to *answer* our prayer; the wonder is that he is able to *hear* it. He is God; we are merely men. He is holy; our sin separates us from him. He is wise; we ask foolishly. He is unchanging; we contradict even our own praying. But in spite of all this we have been able to pray because we have a high priest, even Jesus, who "is passed into the heavens," who intercedes for us. He is that because he became man for us and died on Calvary to bring us back to God. It is this thought that should fill our minds as we rise from our prayer. Every prayer should lead us to a new consciousness of his love in dying for us. A new offering of ourselves and a new submission to his will follows. Thus the dynamic power of the love of Calvary surges into our living and its purpose renews our enthusiasm. Our "Thank you for listening to me" is meaningless if it does not imply "And I will try to do your will."

It is this thought of the immensity of our debt to the Lord which should be uppermost in our minds as we bring our more formal praying to its conclusion. The objective, outward look to God lifts us above our faithless fears and cares and sends us out into the world with a new awareness of God's participation in our living. The Lord can use the life thus yielded to him and brought under his control each day through prayer. Direction by his hand is possible only when we keep in touch with him. Even in the sophisticated control systems of the manned space program constant communication between the space vehicle and mission control is vital. Worship in prayer keeps our lives in daily communication with God. A renewed awareness of his love inspires us to a fuller yielding of ourselves and, consequently, keeps our lives more fully under his control.

> Work shall be prayer, if all be wrought
> As thou wouldst have it done;
> And prayer, by Thee inspired and taught,
> Itself with work be one.

Spontaneous Prayer

Some Christians find that even the simple four-point order of prayer just described requires too much discipline in an area of life in which they are weak. They need help to see that prayer springs from living. They need to be able to talk with God in a free, spontaneous way, to have a conversation with him exactly as if they were talking to their best friend. That is, of course, just what we are doing in prayer. When we forget this fact, prayer is assigned to the "spiritual" corner of our lives and all the rest of our experience is untouched by it.

Talking with God

We need to be able to talk freely with God, as though he were always at our side. Our conversation with him will only be free and happy when we know him well. We can get to know him well just as we do when we learn to know a human friend. When we first meet the stranger, our talk is superficial. Indeed it often costs a real effort to find an opening sentence which may, even then, be a trite comment about the weather! Then we begin to discover a little more about him—where he was raised, what he does for a living, what his hobbies are, and so on. The gathering of these facts helps towards knowing him, but a real knowledge can come only through spending a lot of time with him. It is possible for a Christian to know a lot about his faith and still find that he cannot talk freely to God in conversation prayer. This is due to a failure to spend enough time with him. Life today is busy for everybody. Few have the opportunity of spending long hours of mediation before the Lord. The complications of our social structure, in which we have to live, claim so much of our time that only a fraction of it actually remains under our control. It is impossible for us to contract out of such an existence and it may sound like wishful thinking to suggest that we should spend much time in God's presence. We would like to "choose the better part" and sit at Jesus' feet but the bills have to be paid, the children have to be chauffered, the grass has to be cut. And all our time is gone!

How to Find Time for God

There is a way out of the dilemma. If we make a reappraisal of the things that keep us away from God we shall immediately recognize that these are the things that make life what it is. They are life. Family cares and responsibilities, the compulsions of our daily work, our interests and hobbies, our relationships with others in the vast complexity of modern society, are the things of real living. If God is not interested in them, he is not interested in life. But he proved that he is interested in life when Jesus came down and got involved in it. He saw in all things evidences of God at work, in the flowers and birds, in a carpenter making a yoke, in a woman sweeping her floor to find a coin, in a wedding, and in a death. Because he is concerned about these things, we know that they need not drive us away from him. He can come to us in them. All that we need to do is to recognize his presence. Filling out that phrase "recognize his presence" with significance is part of the thrilling experience of spontaneous prayer.

The basic idea of "spontaneous prayer" is to see God in every activity of our lives. For example, consider two series of incidents that might happen in a day's living, one from a man's point of view and the other from a woman's. The man wakes up. God has watched over him during his sleep and has brought him to a new day. He puts his gratitude into words, speaking them aloud,

"Thank you, God, for watching over me during the night. Thank you for this new day; help me to make the most of it." He drives to his office, "Lord, protect me on this ride and help me to be a considerate driver." When he sits at his desk his prayer may be, "I would work for you today." He asks that his relationship with his colleagues at lunch might be a good testimony to Jesus. When his work is done and he is back home again, he might stop near his door to look at the flower blooming there, "What a beautiful world you have made, Father." Last thing at night, as he looks at the stars, he asks that in the inner space of his life he may know heavenly peace.

His wife begins her day thanking God for the love of her family, but it is not always like that, so she may pray, "Lord, give me patience, your patience, today." When at last the kids have caught the school bus and a strange quiet falls upon the house she prays, "Lord, let my work today make our home a lovely place to live in." Today she drives down to the supermarket, "Help me, God, to make good decisions and spend my money wisely." When her children come home she catches that sudden glimpse of the sheer beauty of a beloved child's face. "My God, what a beautiful, glorious wonder you have put in my child's face!" When finally her day ends, her prayer might well be, "Thank you, God, for the strength you gave me today but give me more tomorrow!"

These examples demonstrate how any person can "practice the presence of God" and have a running conversation with him. There is no need to stop what is being done to kneel down or even to bow the head. The prayer is simply offered in the performance of the act. Recognition of God's help is made with the tool in hand; there is no need to lay it down. The actual language used need not be "prayer" language nor need it be put into theological terms. Use the speech of every day and the natural expressions which would be used with your friends, because prayer is talking with your best friend.

The prayer should not be long. The brief sentence summing up dominant feelings focuses thought and lets God reach us more easily in it. One element must be in each prayer and that is the conscious recognition of God's part in the occasion for our prayer. Any man might say, "What a wonderful view." That will not necessarily bring him nearer to the creator's heart. When we say, "Praise you, Lord, for this wonderful view that you have shown to me," that does. The conscious recognition of the presence of the Lord in all the different scenes and demands of life is that which makes us aware of his presence. He is always near us; we have grown so familiar with his presence that we are no more aware of it than we are of the unceasing beating of the heart. When something happens that makes us feel the heart's beat, we become conscious of it. It so fills our consciousness that we just cannot forget it until some new experience draws the attention of the mind to something else. The deliberate naming of God in the spontaneous prayer draws our attention to him so that we really become aware of his presence and his activity in our living. The constant repetition of this reminder will alert us many times every day to the part that he is playing in our experiences. Thus we shall be more thankful, more responsive to his work for us, more appreciative of his loving care, more ready to turn to him for guidance, more alive spiritually.

The Value of Spontaneous Prayer

The value of conversational prayer cannot be exaggerated. Living with an acute awareness of the presence of the Lord transforms our responses to life. When we face trouble we shall do so with him. The crises of temptation can be overcome when the Savior is near. Choosing between two paths is easier with him to guide. His transforming friendship changes the chore into a privilege and multiplies our enjoyment of the beautiful. We become morally stronger, more alert mentally, and more alive spiritually. All of this is added to the Christian's life by "practicing the presence of God."

When the first attempts are made to practice such conversation prayer, the believer may think that there is little happy spontaneity about it. Those who have used it, however, would agree that though conscious thought and effort have to be invested in it at the beginning, the initial experience is so exciting that after the first few conversation prayers the mind starts to search eagerly for others. When the first conversation prayers have added the new dimension of the depth of God's presence to the little things that go to make up our day, we shall discover that he is present in all sorts of unexpected ways and places. Quite soon the habit is established and prayer becomes joyfully spontaneous. All our "spontaneous" responses are conditioned by that training which builds reflexes and reactions into mind and will. The ball player practices and trains to make his reactions immediate and spontaneous. That astounding curving leap which the footballer makes to catch the pass is the epitome of spontaneity. It is completely unpremeditated. If the player had thought about it at all he would have said, "Can't be done!" But his training has prepared him to make that immediate, unpremeditated, reaction to the play. That is what the Christian does with his prayer until all his life becomes a spontaneous response to God in a song of praise and prayer.

A Testimony

The value of spontaneous prayer is vividly seen in the testimony of Harold Wakeford. Harold is an ordinary countryman who earns his living as a landscape gardener. A few years ago he told his pastor that he was ashamed of being unable to participate verbally in the prayer meeting. The pastor explained the method of the spontaneous prayer to him and Harold decided to put it into practice.

Today Harold regularly enriches the life of his church by his wonderful prayers that come from the heart of a man who knows God. His total usefulness in the Lord has been recognized by his church because just recently, after years of unfruitful membership in the church, he has been elected to be a deacon. His pastor asked him to write a paragraph for the church bulletin to share his experience and encourage others. His testimony is a graphic description of what spontaneous prayer can mean. Harold Wakeford wrote,

"Look deep down into a single flower, stop and stare at the clear blue sky and watch the clouds when they are particularly lovely, stare at the moon until it seems really close . . . hold a young puppy or kitten in your hands, watch lambs playing and, if you can, hold one . . . look at a ploughed field, a horse galloping . . . just stand and stare. And suddenly you will find yourself thinking deeply about all these things—and you will realize that you have really been praying and, indeed, worshiping God who made all these things and millions of others. He is such a wonderful craftsman, and craftsmen just like their handicraft to be admired and being thanked for them. So there you are. In no time at all the make-up of your prayer will become so varied that you will find yourself getting deeper and deeper into conversation with God. And then you will know what prayer really is."

Using a Prayer List

One Sunday the pastor was greeting his people at the door as they left after worship. When Mrs. Brown stood in front of him she said, "I would like to thank you, pastor, for what you have done for my family during the past few weeks." The pastor used a series of polite sayings as he frantically searched his memory for a recollection of *anything* that he had done for this woman or her family. The woman heard his words but his eyes told her that he was bewildered. "You've forgotten all about it!" she exclaimed. "Three weeks ago you promised to pray for my husband during surgery."

How easy it is to forget the promises we make so easily. If we are going to keep our promises to others and to ourselves we shall do well to keep a written list of requests that we may use in the "asking" time of our prayer.

Setting Up a Simple Prayer List

Prayer lists may be nothing more than a list of names written down on a scrap of paper. In their complete simplicity these can be very helpful. The names of our family members and friends do not escape our loving thought, but the prayer list will keep before us that great crowd of people who need our prayer or who do not know how to pray for themselves.

From time to time the prayer list may be used to see whether our prayer is wide enough. It will show us how far our concern is reaching beyond the circle of our relatives and friends to others in great need. If it shows a deficiency, we are challenged to extend it and reach out to a world of people. The person who really believes in prayer will never want that mighty power to be used only for the intimate personal concerns of his little circle. He will find so many claims jostling for a place in his prayer list that he will be glad to have it as a means of marshalling his thought before talking to the Lord about it all. He will want to remember every section of his church's work, not just that area in which he works. Names and issues will come from contacts with the neighborhood, at school, at work, from leisuretime associations and so on. Overseas missionary magazines will provide lists of missionaries' names and the places where they are working. The daily newspaper will often tell stories that will attract our attention and move our hearts.

When persons and issues like this move us and so find their way into our enlarging prayer life, we do need to be selective. If we try to pray for everybody in the telephone directory, or every sad story that we read in the newspaper, our prayer will obviously become so diffuse that it will be unreal. We have to choose a few names and issues about which we can pray with consistency and intelligence. The work of selecting individuals and subjects for the list actually increases a sense of responsibility to show the spirit of Christ in witness and ministry to everyone we meet in all parts of our life. When our daily prayer is filled with a wider love, that wider love will warm our response to the needs of the people we meet in the course of the day. The experience of such prayer will wonderfully increase belief in prayer and strengthen the Christian life.

Using a More Advanced Prayer List

These goals can be achieved more rapidly and effectively by employing a more advanced style of prayer list. The simple type just described will be all that many people will want but others will find a more developed tool most profitable in their spiritual growth. This "tool" is a help in looking for the answers God gives to prayer in addition to being a means of disciplining our requests. It is frustrating to write a letter and get no answer; it is soul destroying to pray for something of serious concern and then miss God's response. The advanced list encourages the Christian to be constant and disciplined in the asking side of his prayer and, at the same time, it has a built-in help to keep him alert for the answer which God never fails to give.

The list consists of four columns, two broad columns for details about prayer requests and two narrow ones for dates. The narrow columns are for the dates and the wider columns are for notes about prayer matters. Head the first and third columns "Date," head the second column "Prayer Request" and the fourth column "Answer."

When prayer for a person or issue is begun the date is written in column 1, followed by a brief definition of the prayer in column 2. As constant prayer is offered the remaining empty columns are a daily reminder that we are expecting an answer. Go on praying faithfully until the Lord answers. At that time the date is written in column 3 and the answer is briefly described in column 4.

It is always difficult for the average Christian to "keep on praying." The list of prayer requests will keep before our minds those things that we have felt sufficiently serious about to commit them to paper in a resolve to go on praying about them. The list will challenge us when we feel like giving up because of lack of faith, or because there seems an impossible delay, or simply because we get tired. The column headed "Answer" will also encourage us. When we are expecting a reply to a letter, the mailbox stands like a sentinel guarding our confidence that an answer will come. Every time we see it we ask, "Has the mailman brought a reply today?" and we go out expectantly to see. The four-column prayer list performs this function for the prayer life.

Sometimes the answer to that letter comes by telephone! We are just as ready to accept it this way; what we want is an answer. The fact that God does not always answer prayer in the anticipated form is frequently overlooked. This undermines faith because of the feeling that since the Father did not apparently answer our prayer, prayer does not work. He has answered though. But we have not heard. This prayer list challenges us to look for answers whenever and however they come. When the answer comes, a brief description, with the date, is written in the reply columns. This list teaches us both to speak and to listen to God as we pray.

God always answers our prayers and he never answers no. If prayer is not in line with his will he will say, "No, but . . ." and then will offer some better thing beyond the wisdom and expectation of the original prayer. This was Paul's experience. He prayed often for "the thorn in the flesh" to be taken away. The answer he received was a "No, but . . ." The Lord said, "No, but . . . my grace is sufficient for you." It may have been hard for Paul to hear that no but it led him to one of his deepest insights and proudest boasts. "Most gladly therefore will I rather glory in my infirmities, that the power of Christ may rest upon me" (2 Cor. 12:9).

Prayer is not like an automatic machine which produces exactly what is ordered when the button is pushed. The person of God enters into it. He knows better than we what we ought to pray for, so when we open our hearts to him he will sometimes deny us the precise things we ask for because he wants us to have a different, but a better, thing. Too often when he answers with something different we just do not notice it. The column for answers will keep the mind and heart sensitive to the will and activity of God. When we are really looking for his answer, we shall find it, sometimes in surprising but always in satisfying acts.

If the believer keeps a prayer list, he will provide for himself a thrilling account of growth in his spiritual pilgrimage. Each line will be an encouraging testimony, built from his own experience of God's fatherly care. It will thrill him with the rich generosity and the endlessly varied expressions of his grace that the Lord is always showing toward us.

PART
4

How Can I Grow Through Worship?

PART

4

Is Worship Important?

Jesus thought that regular worship was of top importance. He himself went to the synagogue every sabbath. Luke tells us that he went into the synagogue in Nazareth on the sabbath day "as was his custom." We know that the home in which he was raised was faithful in its observance of the customs of Judaism. The child Jesus was presented in the Temple on his eighth day (Luke 2:21ff) and, when he was twelve years old, Mary and Joseph took him to Jerusalem when they made their annual visit for the Passover (Luke 2:41ff). His own familiarity with the Temple and its customs shows that he entered fully into worship practices of Judaism and taught his disciples to do so too.

There is, however, very little recorded about any teaching that Jesus may have offered about this aspect of the Christian life. This is surprising because it is certain that from the very earliest times the disciples met, as Christians, to worship. The opening chapters of the book of Acts pictures a church which was regularly meeting together for Christian praise and prayer, apart from any religious practices that they continued as Jews. The letters of Paul reflect the activities of the church in its earliest years and they clearly show that the believers came together in Christian groups for worship. The 1 Corinthian letter is particularly useful for this. Paul gives a thumbnail sketch of worship in that church when he writes, "When you come together, each one has a hymn, a lesson, a revelation, a tongue, or an interpretation" (1 Cor. 14:26, RSV).

This shows that the main elements of our own church worship, hymn, prayer, and lesson, were already combined together in the worship pattern of the primitive church. Paul also indicates that the remembrance of the Lord's Supper was part of their reason for assembling together (1 Cor. 11:17f). The writer of the Hebrews letter exhorts his readers to be faithful in their worship practices: "Not forsaking the assembling of ourselves together as the manner of some is" (Heb. 10:25).

Records of the church in the period just after New Testament days show how firmly worship practices were established. They never urge the importance of them upon members; they simply clarify what ought to be done. For instance, in the *Didache,* an ancient document of the church going back to about the year 100, the writer gives the instruction, "And on the Lord's day of the Lord come together and break bread and give thanks." The document gives detailed instructions for the way to conduct baptismal services, the Lord's Supper, and the practice of regular fasting. It shows that the Lord's Prayer was regularly repeated by all worshipers in the assembly.

Pliny, who was an administrator of the province of North Africa in the Roman Empire, wrote to the Emperor Trajan in about the year 112, "On a stated day they [the Christians] had been accustomed to come together before daybreak and to recite a hymn among themselves to Christ, as though he were a god." This reference is important because it takes us right out of Judaism and gives evidence, in an official government paper, how the worship practices of the church had been established and were positively directed to the person of Jesus Christ himself. Visitors to present-day Rome are made very conscious of this when they visit the catacombs. In those underground tunnels, two thousand years ago, in the midst of persecutions designed by Roman emperors to stamp out the Christian faith, believers met secretly for worship. They wrote on the cave walls symbols such as the cross, alpha and omega, and the sign of the fish, all of which have found their way permanently into the symbolism of church worship.

There is no period in the Church's history that indicates that Christians could ever grow in spiritual life or service without the practice of formal worship. All over the Mediterranean and North European countries it is possible to trace the rise and fall of Christianity by the remains of church buildings, which provide us with a history in stone. Significantly most of those remains are of worship sanctuaries. Even when the church divided and split into various groups and factions they all continued to worship. The fundamental changes of the Reformation were based on deep divisions of interpretation of the Scriptures and of the practice of the Christian faith, but in both the old tradition, continued in Roman Catholicism, and the new faith, expressed in Protestantism, worship remained central. Among Martin Luther's most precious gifts to us are some splendid hymns. A study of the hymns used in any Christian church today will show how men of many different traditions have put their praise and worship into hymns that have proved acceptable to people worshiping in other traditions.

Even when the Quaker movement grew up in Protestantism united worship was not abandoned. This is surprising because George Fox and his followers stressed the importance of the Inner Light, the personal revelation granted within a man's spirit by the work of the Holy Spirit. Though Fox magnified personal devotion, he encouraged the Quakers to come together in the Meeting House, and in silence, to wait upon the Lord. Sometimes individuals were led to share thoughts that had been given to them, sometimes they would pray aloud, but often a whole meeting hour would pass in unbroken silence. The silence would, however, be a shared act of unified worship in the presence of God. It was pregnant with a power that resulted in action in the world outside.

In the decline of church influence at the present time there are many who think that they can worship individually outside the life of the church. There are many who think that the assembly of worship is an empty formality which adds nothing to life's meaning and purpose. Later we shall consider certain activities of devotion as they are exercised in individual and group worship. At this point we would stress that, whether it be in a congregation singing antiphonally in an ancient church in Milan or Salvationists singing choruses to the accompaniment of their brass band on a street corner in the East End of London, Christians have felt a compulsion to worship together.

And this they have felt for two reasons. In the first place they have felt the immensity and holiness of their God which has required them to bow before him. He is God. Therefore they must worship. Their worship must be a worship in togetherness, for the acknowledgement of his reality in ordinary life sets the believer apart from the unbeliever. In the community of those who share his faith he is better able to pour out his heart to God and to give him that praise which springs upon from within the worshiping heart. The psalmist's cry, "Enter his gates with praise," is echoed by the apocalyptist's song, "Worthy art thou to receive praise," and so the song goes round the earth and along the passages of time as men rise up and feel it a vital part of their life together to turn their gaze upon the one to whom all men owe the debt of life. Objectively Christians have been constrained to join in communal worship to find the adequate expression of their worship longings.

This leads to the second reason why worship has been a constant feature of Christian life through the centuries; it is man's own need of being lifted above himself. The objective expression of worship has a subjective result. Worship lifts a man outside himself as he turns to adore his God. It strengthens him from within because his worship makes him more sensitive to the Spirit's work. It places him in the fellowship of worshiping Christians from whom he derives inspiration and encouragement. A worshiping man finds that worship lifts the weight of his responsibilities and anxieties; it multiplies and substantiates his joys.

Worship, whether individual or communal, puts power into the living of the moral Christian life. We become like that which we worship without any external compulsion. Our attempts at emulation—whether it be the dress or hairstyle of a favorite music star, the style of our favorite pitcher, the composure of our favorite actor, or the mannerisms of our favorite preacher—will be sustained of our own volition for just so long as we maintain our hero-worship attitude. When we adore and worship Christ we want to be like him, not because we must but because we ourselves long for it. And in the adoration of worship the power of the Spirit is added to our own subjective desire to give it permanence and power. Worship can set us free from the burden of the law, "Thou shalt . . . ," to know the motivation of grace, "Thou canst . . ." This difference marks the distinction between the conscientious Christian who, unhappily, observes the standards of the gospel because he thinks he ought to and the saintly man who gladly expresses them because he really wants to do so. The secret of joyful living is found in living for one who is adored, Jesus Christ our Lord. The fact that our love for him (in common with all our loves!) is not constant requires that we should seek some influence outside ourselves to help us to maintain it. This is part of the function of communal worship. This builds up a habit of worship which carries us through days of little spiritual impetus. It opens the coolness of our hearts to the enthusiasm and faith of others, who can help us through the doldrums and get us moving again. The Christian who would keep on growing will not neglect the assembly of his fellow-believers.

4

Growing in Individual Personal Worship

The Christian faith is a faith that comes to fruition in fellowship and, especially, in the fellowship of worship. This should not lead us to the assumption that we can grow spiritually only in worship with others. On the contrary, there are times when we need to draw apart by ourselves to turn our thought upon the Lord in personal adoration and worship.

Much has been written in the two preceding chapters on the place of spontaneous prayer and daily Bible reading in the individual life. These are two of the major elements of our regular personal worship. Worship is the turning of the heart's adoration outward to the God in whom we believe. When we take the Bible, read it as God's own inspired word, and then apply it to ourselves in the question, "What would God say to me through this passage so that I may obey him?" we are truly involved in worship. When, in spontaneous prayer we praise him, deliberately naming him, for some very beautiful thing that we experience, that is worship. Worship of this sort, so closely linked with life, really does glorify God for it produces, on the one hand, ready obedience and imitation, and on the other, adoration flowing out to him in free praise.

Spontaneous prayer and Bible reading do not cover all that can be done to encourage growth through private, personal worship. It is possible, for instance, to set aside some time during a leisure day or on a vacation for a period of fellowship with and meditation upon God. Let's imagine that we are to have the privilege of spending a vacation in the Holy Land. We shall plan our trip so that we may spend time in some of those places dear and familiar to us because of their associations with the Lord. It is certain that we would not go around, camera over our shoulders, guidebook in hand and a determined look in the eye that would say, "We're gonna see everything, just everything, honey!" That might be fine for London town but we all recognize that in the place where Jesus walked we have to tread softly, Bible in hand, to meditate and worship. The wild flowers in Galilee will make us want to hear, ". . . even Solomon in all his glory . . . ," that steep unpaved street lined with slender cypress trees will make us pause and remember in Bethany, "Jesus wept. . . . Behold how he loved." The garden tomb, the excavated house in Emmaus, will stop our haste again to hear that cry, "The Lord is risen indeed!" In such places personal worship would come easily.

That type of vacation may not be for everybody, but that does not mean that we cannot worship in the same way in another land, in a very different type of leisure opportunity. By the Grand Canyon with its palette of color and its canvass of strange, ever-changing shapes; by the roar of Niagara, with its pounding, ceaseless power; under the Spanish moss in the romance of an historic southland; by the rugged coasts of New England or the silver, palm-fringed beaches of Florida; among the peaks of the Rockies or under the broad horizon-spanning sky of the prairies, we can meet him. Or maybe in the meadow by the creek, or on the bank of the local reservoir, or in our own yard sweet with the scent of the honeysuckle clinging to the mailbox, we can find him best. There is a place where, with deliberate intent, we can draw aside for a while, in the middle of the hectic rush of life, to be quiet with God. We need such time in these busy, worldly days when we are pressed by demands so difficult to satisfy. The daily time of prayer and meditation is an oasis of refreshment in the daily round. But we have need sometimes to take a little more time to refresh ourselves and build up our strength for the journey.

What can we do then? In planning for that vacation we can plan to take along spiritual aids just as we take along "fun" aids. Pack the fishing rods and swim suits into the car but do not forget the Bible and any book that may be helpful in drawing nearer to the Lord. Such books might be selected from Christian biographies, or from books on Bible background, or on spiritual maturity, or on Christian thinking—something spiritually helpful that the demands of life, including our church service, usually prevent our reading. The reading of such a book through the vacation can be used as a prompter of realistic worship experiences. Additionally, it may be helpful, as the itinerary is planned, to anticipate allowing time in some beautiful or quiet place for sincere meditation on our relationship to God and our fellows. Many popular vacation centers (such as Calloway Gardens in Georgia and Knott's Berry Farm near Los Angeles) actually provide little chapels in places of beauty to help in this.

We should not overlook the fact that there are other times when we are busy with all the normal activities of heavy schedules, when we need time for God to speak to us. This does happen in church on Sunday and in our daily devotions. Occasions will, however, often arise when we shall need more time for personal worship. Let us notice some examples. The parents of a child will often praise God spontaneously for their little one and they will early seek to tell stories of Jesus to him. The privilege of parenthood requires wisdom, patience, love, faith, and these need cultivation in a time of worship when parents have time to thank God for the gift and seek guidance in their duties. The doctor will pray before he operates, but he needs to set time aside also for giving praise to the Lord for the wonders of man's dedicated skills and for trying to understand the value of human life from the viewpoint of his creator. The person who feels that he has a dull, routine job that anybody could do needs to break out of the routine to see his place in the scheme of God's mighty plan. "He that is faithful in that which is least is faithful also in much" (Luke 16:10). In times of deep experience, joyful and sad, extra time set apart for the Lord's worship will increase the joy and keep us humble! It will solace our sadness and deepen our trust.

It is good to offer these times of worship to our God on our own, or at most, with one other person. Our contact with God in the deeper, intimate crises of life and death must be in the singular; there are things we inevitably face alone. If we can build up our ability to worship him when we are alone, we shall never be alone, without him, not even in those greatest tests of faith which every mortal finally faces.

Growing in Worship with Others at Church

The church which we attend may be seen as the place where we gather as God's people around an altar or we may see it as a place where the Lord's people gather like a family to meet their Father. The church with the altar is more like the temple; the other is more like a family home. The former type is usually associated with the Roman Catholic, Episcopalian, "Church"-type churches whilst the latter is usually associated with the more evangelical, Baptist, Church of Christ, "sect"-type churches. It is to people of the latter type of church that these comments will most fully apply. Worshipers in such churches do not believe in the mediation of a priesthood nor do they believe that any altar is necessary in the sanctuary for the offering has been made once and for all upon Calvary.

The importance of stressing this distinction is seen immediately on entering churches of the different types for Sunday worship. In the "sect" type of church there is great informality as friend greets friend and, though some may criticize it, there is often a whisper of conversation across the church. If this gets so loud that it destroys any spirit of worship, then the criticism is justified, but if it is restrained and quiet, it is indeed part of our coming together for worship. We come as a family. We are going to sing praise together. We shall remember each other's needs in prayer. We shall read the Bible and think about it personally but together. How good it is to be with fellow-believers! How we need to share in this fellowship, one with another, as we come to meet one who is our heavenly Father and whose wondrous love in the Son we have experienced in different ways. It is therefore understandable that we should want to share, in the happiness of being together in the family of God, the many things that go to make up our ordinary living as we greet each other with the word of interest, or encouragement, or of congratulation. As the choir enters, or as the organ plays a prelude to worship, it is helpful for the individual worshiper to turn his attention to worship. Though he comes into the presence of one who loves him deeply he is coming before the presence of the Most High God. Moments should be spent in silent, thoughtful prayer, preparing the heart for the Spirit's movement, eagerly anticipating a new understanding of the Savior's love, praying that some may be helped and others saved. The heart prepared is a heart open to the Lord. Pray for the people who will lead the worship—the music director, the singers, the preacher—and ask that they may be voices of the Lord, filled with his love and power. Expect things to happen in the worship service!

The Music

Most of the active participation of the worshiper in our worship services is achieved through the singing of hymns. The first hymns in a service should be hymns of praise and then will follow songs chosen to express, describe, develop aspects of Christian experience. The final hymn of the service will usually be of the invitation type which will aid the people in coming to some resolution for their living.

It is sad to see many people in the congregation standing listlessly through the hymns, making no attempt to join in them. We can grow in worship through the singing of hymns. From the very earliest days of the Christian church believers have sung to their Lord. And it is reasonable that they should. When we feel happy we sing; when something good has happened to us we rejoice. When we have won a victory we want to join in noisy chorus. That is what the Lord's people do when they sing songs in praise of Jesus. He is so precious and wonderful that we simply must tell it continuously in song and music. The joy of the Christian is best expressed this way and John Newton gets to the heart of the matter when he joyously writes,

> When we've been there ten thousand years,
>   Bright shining as the sun,
> We've no less days to sing God's praise
>   Than when we first begun.

We must emphasize that this act of participation in the hymn of praise is itself a growth experience. In ordinary life we know how a word of thanks or appreciation can bring us nearer to the person who has served us. The putting of our thanks into words makes our appreciation grow. So with hymns. Most of us have only limited powers of imagination and we find it hard to discover new and effective ways of praise. So we turn to words written by inspired poets and musicians across two thousand years and we make their experiences ours as we lift up the heart in song. That is a growing experience indeed and, even though we may have no voice that will blend harmoniously into the praise of the congregation, the reading of the words and some contemplation on their meaning, as others add the depth of music to the written word, will carry us beyond our poor experience into a richer one.

Another reason why we should sing the hymns in the worship service is that they are teaching aids. The Wesley brothers understood the importance of this aspect of hymn-singing. The glorious hymns of Charles have all that objectivity, praise to God for his own sake that hymns need to have, but he was also able to capture in his poetry much theological teaching.

A vast storehouse of Christian understanding and experience has been opened to all who have sung his hymns. Very many of the people who first came to the Lord under John Wesley's preaching were illiterate and, initially, could not read their Bibles. Charles helped them to grasp the fundamentals of the faith in words and tunes easily remembered. For example, think of all the theology compressed into his stanza

> His death is my plea;
> My Advocate see,
> And hear the blood speak that hath answered for me:
> He purchased the grace
> Which now I embrace
> O Father, thou knowest he hath died in my place!

The person who learns this by heart has the basic principles of the plan of salvation (or the doctrine of the atonement) firmly fixed in his mind. Similarly Toplady's hymn, "Rock of Ages," written around the same time, has taught thousands of Christians that the cross of Jesus deals not only with the guilt of sin but also with its power.

> Let the water and the blood,
> From thy wounded side which flowed,
> Be of sin the double cure,
> Save from wrath and make me pure.

Edwin Hatch's two great hymns on the work of the Holy Spirit, "Breathe on Me, Breath of God" and "Holy Spirit, Breathe on Me" have taught many generations of Christians what to expect of the work of the Holy Spirit.

Other hymns have helped in the development of the devotional life.

> Oh what peace we often forfeit.
> Oh, what needless pain we bear,
> All because we do not carry
> Ev'rything to God in prayer!

When Joseph Scriven shared these thoughts in the hymn "What a Friend We Have in Jesus" he made a gift to every believer of the most helpful thought that when we have taken our hopes, fears, problems, griefs, to the Lord in prayer we do not need to go on carrying them around. If this is a familiar thought to the reader, it is undoubtedly because this very hymn has made the truth clear in a movingly memorable poetic statement. Devotional hymns have taken people through all the crises of life and have helped many a man down the bank of Jordan, the divide between this life and the next. Many a saint has passed into victory on the words of John Newton,

> How sweet the name of Jesus sounds
> In a believer's ear!
> It soothes his sorrows, heals his wounds,
> And drives away his fear.

Our hymnbooks are treasure stores of devotion but they are powerhouses too. From them we can derive help from the experience of wonderful Christians of many generations, nations and branches of the Christian church. But not if we sit in the pew, hymnbook and mouth shut, with our minds wandering from the hairstyle of the woman sitting in front of us, to what restaurant we should go to for lunch when the service has ground to a stop, to the fish (or the bargain!) that got away. This is to neglect one of the most helpful aids to growth which the Lord has prepared for his rejoicing people.

Closely allied with the praise of our congregational hymn singing is the service rendered by the choir. Their contribution can be really significant if we see it as an offering to God of music that is better than that which the congregation as a whole can bring. It is unfortunate that the "special music" has dropped to the level of an item in a performance in many churches. It should be seen as an attempt to bring the best that we have to that Lord whom angels and archangels praise in glory. Those less gifted in the arts of music can listen and be caught up into magnificence of the glory of the chorus or be identified with the depth of personal testimony of the soloist. Poor is that worshiper who has not grown as he has heard the choir sing, whether it be a Handel chorus or a Sankey hymn!

The Prayers

What is the significance that prayer holds when we join in it as a congregation? Jesus had a significant contribution to make here for he taught that prayer has extra power when believers gather together and, with one accord, pray to their Father. He said, "If two of you agree on earth as touching anything that they shall ask, it shall be done to them of my Father which is in heaven." The joining together in love and faith adds significance to the prayer. This has undoubtedly been the experience of many through the years as they have seen the wonderful effects of prayer in worshiping communities. Prayer unites a community and that contributes to each member's growth. Prayer also helps a community to attempt to answer its own prayers! When a group of people, who are concerned about staffing the Sunday School for instance, pray together about it, it is more likely that one of them may feel a constraint to volunteer or, at least, decide to make a definite approach to some person about it. The place of the prayer meeting in our tradition cannot be overestimated. It has been the source of tremendous power and it may be asserted that when its position is restored (as a meeting to which people go really to wrestle with the Lord in prayer) we shall see greater power and joy flowing into church life. Individuals who constitute such a prayer meeting are persons who grow. They grow in their spiritual stature, in service to the Lord and in commitment to his church.

This same thing happens in the ordinary Sunday service. There the whole assembly of the church joins together in prayer, sometimes led by the pastor or someone on whom he calls. In comparison with the written prayers of more formal services these prayers are neither as beautiful in their language nor as carefully thought out but they do have the important advantage of being closely linked with the life of the church, being spontaneous and free. Frequently prayer requests described by members will be included in such prayer. Much could be done very easily to enrich the quality of these prayers and make them more helpful in the worship experience. They are usually far too repetitious (because little thought or feeling is put into them). If Bible-believing Christians would draw upon the countless ideas that the Bible contains about the truth and relevance of our faith and employ the rich language of the Bible-imagery, prayer in the assembly would certainly inspire and uplift much more than it does in most churches today. Having recognized this point, however, it remains true that when a whole congregation really participates in love in such united prayer the whole is blessed. If the whole is blessed, then the individuals who make up the group are too. This love of the Lord and our fellows, in finding expression in prayer, deepens and enriches the experience of the growing Christian.

The difficulty is sometimes raised that we cannot intelligently participate in congregational prayer because we do not know what is going to be said in the prayer. There are two points to be made in reference to this. First, when we go to a meeting of our own church we know much about its life, people, ideals, problems. We have become familiar with the type of service that is held and the way in which our fellow-members pray. Therefore, with knowledge and familiarity it is easy for us to follow the prayer with understanding. Second, prayer is conversation, a believer talking to his Lord. When someone talks to us we are able to follow what is being said and, in the majority of instances, we are able to anticipate what is going to be said. We recognize the line of thought and our minds run ahead of the words of the person who is performing the slower tasks of thinking and talking. There is no reason why we should not be able to do the same in prayer and be able to pray with the person who is offering a spontaneous prayer. Unity of this sort in prayer is a common experience and in itself is a wonderfully reassuring experience of the oneness of the body of Christ. A deliberate attempt to think in step with the person praying should be made by anyone who has difficulty in joining in the prayer of the church service. It will enlarge appreciation of one's fellow members, it will extend the vision and it will fill the heart with new love for God and man.

The Reading of the Bible

Many people who take their Bibles to Sunday School forget to use them during the reading of the Bible in the preaching service. It is a good habit to follow the public reading in the worshiper's own Bible. This helps to concentrate attention on the Scripture passage and avoids some of those distractions which may divert attention. It may be helpful to follow in a modern version, though this can be confusing if the version is too different from that being used in the pulpit. If the preacher reads from the King James Version it may be good to read the Revised Standard Version with him. This translation is sufficiently close to the King James Version to make it easy to see where the reader is but, at the same time, it puts the thoughts into modern, quickly comprehensible language. Of course, with very familiar passages it is easy to follow in any of the new translations and receive from them fresh insights in the familiar verses.

Christians inherited the practice of reading the Scriptures together from the practice of the Jewish synagogue. It has been a feature of Christian worship from the very beginning and reminds the worshiper of the fact that God has given us a guide for our personal and church conduct. When the reading is undertaken with previous preparation and thought, the worshiper is certainly helped by it. Many chapters have come to life with a new significance as someone has read the words, and after prayerful consideration of them, has imparted to them something of his own understanding. This enlarges understanding for the person following the reading and is a means of growth.

Perhaps the greatest help comes when the Bible reading is

chosen for its value as background material for the sermon. The preacher should make it a general rule to read from the chapter from which his sermon is taken or some other passage which will help the hearer more completely understand his message. This preparation helps the worshiper make a more rapid stride of comprehension as the sermon begins and consequently makes the preached word more effective.

Through the tradition of the reading of the Scriptures in church there has been only one change in method and that was introduced in Milan by Bishop Ambrose, when the city was under siege and many people had taken refuge in the cathedral. He divided the congregation into two parts. Each part read a verse of Scripture in turn, antiphonally. Some present-day churches follow a similar custom in the responsive reading. A psalm or a chapter of the Bible is read responsively, the pastor taking one verse and the congregation the next. Some hymnbooks have collections of responsive readings, selections of verses from various parts of the Bible developing some theme. This method of reading secures excellent participation from the worshipers and can make a real contribution to their understanding of the worship.

The Sermon

The sermon is traditionally central in worship in Baptist, Methodist, Presbyterian, and certain other Protestant churches. In the pulpit the preacher enters into the line of the prophets who declared, "Thus saith the Lord . . ." In this activity we apply the belief that the Holy Spirit continues to direct and inspire his servants and we are fully justified in describing the sermon by the word "message."

In making preparation for his pulpit ministry the preacher will have prayed for guidance. The topic may have been given to him as a result of his pastoral experience, it may have been suggested by a question raised in his reading, or it may have come through his own personal devotions in private prayer and Bible reading.

It is a thrilling privilege for the pastor to go to his pulpit believing that he is no other than God's messenger for the hour and if he has the further confidence that his people believe the same thing, then wings will be added to his words. If we do not believe that the Lord can direct the preacher's work, then we certainly need to rethink our whole attitude to worship. If we do believe that the Lord can still use a man as his ambassador, we ought to judge the sermon by that standard and not by the standards of length, novelty, or personality.

The growing Christian will find that the sermon can do a great many things for him. For centuries the pulpit was the only teaching medium that the church used. A well-prepared preacher can teach a congregation a great deal about the Lord and his ways, the Book and its revelation, and about man and his life. While the pulpit should never be solely a teacher's desk, the element of teaching will always be there and we should listen for it. A sermon may develop a moral theme, underlining our responsibilities to practice what the gospel preaches in individual and community living. It may be a word of comfort and solace, drawing upon the assurances of God's word in building up his people. It may contain the note of challenge to greater commitment and vision. Many sermons are inspirational and send a man on his way rejoicing in the Lord. Yet others may be designed to motivate a man to fuller service. Some will be prepared as a result of the pastor's longing to see his people growing in their knowledge of God and what he has done for his people. A majority of sermons will be preached to secure decisions for Christ. Every sermon should be preached to produce some result. We grow in grace as we listen to God's authentic word in it and seek to respond.

Every preacher will know that very frequently God does things with his sermons that the preacher never anticipated in the writing of them. Every word spoken to us has to be translated according to our own understanding of the word. This interpretation will unavoidably be influenced by the circumstances of our own life and thinking. Add to this our belief that the Holy Spirit's work can open minds and souls and it becomes clear that one word going out from the pulpit means as many different things as there are people in the congregation. The same sermon may, to the preacher's glad surprise, be used of the Lord to comfort a sorrowing person or to challenge another faced with a critical decision or to reprimand yet another who has done some backsliding. But none of these results follow if the learner simply hears only the words of a man. "Lord, what do you want to say to me today? Give me an understanding mind and a responsive heart so that I may learn more about you," is a prayer which we should all make our own as the preacher takes up the serious task of opening the word of God.

People find it exceedingly hard to maintain concentration at a high level over the time taken to preach a sermon. The best preachers recognize this and use various devices to relax the audience, to give the hearers a fresh line of thinking, to attract the wandering attention. The listener can play his part in working to keep up his concentration. At the lowest levels these suggestions may relieve the boredom of a sermon or, at the highest, may be the means of opening ears to what the Lord would speak.

The person who is really eager to develop a skill in listening to sermons will attempt to make written notes. While such notes do give the opportunity for the serious listener to go through the thoughts of the sermon a second time, this is not the chief purpose in making them. The chief purpose is to employ the hand and the eye in the learning experience, to support the work of the ear by an involvement of the other senses. Nothing elaborate is needed—a sheet of paper placed in the Bible, or a small notebook in the pocket, and something to write with is all that is needed. The notes are not intended to be so detailed that a report of the sermon could be written from them. They are notes which will help the hearer to follow the thought-steps which the preacher takes. More detailed notes may be made on points which are particularly challenging or helpful. The actual exercise of writing the notes serves to maintain continuity of concentration but, more than that, the writing helps us hold the thoughts more clearly. We remember what we write much longer than the things which we hear.

A basic knowledge of the principles of sermon construction will help in the making of notes. All sermons are different and every preacher has his own method of writing a sermon. There are, however, some things which can be said in general about sermon construction. Every sermon should have an introduction and a conclusion. The introduction will be planned to arouse interest, to identify the area of thought or to indicate the method that is going to be used. In most sermons it will be brief. The house has only a small porch. In the conclusion the speaker may review what he has said. He may seek to gather it all together in a closing thought. He will certainly strive to gain a response to the message from the hearer. This will require some decision or resolve to live the life more fully. Many sermons will conclude with a definite invitation to decision for Christ in first commitment or in renewal of dedication to him. This may include the invitation to walk the aisle in token of decision. This act strengthens the person who does it and is also an inspiration to all who witness it. No sermon should be planned with the sole aims of informing or entertaining. No sermon should be listened to without the complementary preparedness on the hearer's part to make a response in his life.

Between introduction and conclusion lies the main body of the sermon. This will consist of several points. In the days of C. H. Spurgeon the sermon often consisted of as many as twenty points. Today the preacher may have four but he will seldom go beyond three. There are good reasons for this three-point style of sermon. In the first place, it is impossible for the ordinary listener to remember many points. In fact, the preacher will be happy if his hearer remembers one idea! And this is why his sermon will usually fall into three points developing one theme. The basis of logical reasoning is found in three stages. First of all there is the beginning statement *(the thesis)*. Against this is put another idea, in advance of the first or expressing a contrary point of view *(the antithesis)*. The third stage of reasoning is to unite these two ideas in a resulting new idea *(the synthesis)*. This pattern is basic to most thinking and therefore affects the pattern of the sermon. A very simple example, on Romans 5, might be:

1. Jesus died for sinful men
2. We are sinful men
3. Jesus died for us

This logical form of the three points may not be as evident when the preacher takes a verse and expounds it stage by stage. A simple example might be on John 1:1,14: "In the beginning was the Word . . . and the Word was made flesh and dwelt among us."

1. Jesus was the Word, really God
2. Jesus came in the flesh, really man
3. We can meet God in Christ

Some sermons, while following the three-point form, will not demonstrate the logical development of reasoned argument but may, for instance, offer the repetition of an idea in three different forms.

1. Jesus is the Way
2. Jesus is the Truth
3. Jesus is the Life

As we listen to the sermons of our own pastor, week after week, we shall soon recognize his style and will be able to anticipate how he is going to treat his subject. This will add to our interest and also to our assimilation of his message. We shall be fascinated to see if we can think with him. When we do so we shall be pleased and we shall receive some confirmation of our own thinking. When we do not we shall have the interest of his particular treatment to add to our thought. As we make notes, this will further strengthen the impression and we shall find that the sermon is making a bigger impact upon our lives.

The Personal Consequences of Group Worship

When we have developed skills in these elements of Christian worship, we can really benefit from worship with others. As Christians, we believe that while we can worship God on our own worship with others adds a quality to worship that makes communal worship an imperative for the Christian life.

One of our Lord's most precious promises is, "Where two or three are gathered together in my name, there am I in the midst." Though the Lord is present in the secret place of private worship, he has promised to be most wonderfully present when we meet with others who love him. Though it is exceedingly difficult logically to explain why this is so, most Christians know from experience that it is so. The Christian faith is not a solitary faith. Christians love to be together and, in a special way, they love to be together in worship.

It is a great encouragement to know that the believer is not alone in his witness in a world which may be hostile to him. In the congregation he is reminded that there are many others who share his faith and rejoice in being part of the family of God. Paul's great chapters in the 1 Corinthian letter, on the relationship of each member of the body, is a real help in understanding the relationship between each member of the church to the whole. The truth of this illustration is seen in many activities of the church, including worship.

In worship the individual is strengthened by sharing the faith of others. Obviously he receives much from those who put their faith into words in the leading of worship from both pulpit and choir. But this is by no means all! In worship he enters into the faith and experience of all who worship with him. Each man travels his own road but on the way he has experiences very like those of other men. What he experienced, how he found peace, gained the victory, endured pain, resisted temptation, remained patient through disappointment, and so on, is a help to us when we face our own challenging circumstances. Look at the variety of people in the pews. Glory in the fact that God has shown himself to them in wonderful ways, in a whole world of different experiences, and strength is added to our own souls. This is particularly true of the worshiper in the small church. He may miss something in not having the inspiration of the great crowd and, maybe, the sermon may not be as good as that in the big church, but he can know about the trials of his fellows and the glorious victories God has granted to them. This is so helpful in worship. We are strengthened by shared faith. When our faith burns low, what an inspiration it is to be uplifted by the faith of fellow-worshippers!

What other people do for us in worship we can do for them. When we are seen regularly in our place, others will notice and will be helped to be regular. When it is clear that we are really participating in the worship through hymn, prayer, reading, and sermon, then other people will discover the value of these things. As we take our joys and sorrows to the life of the family in worship, they will receive a blessing from our presence. Many a preacher, for instance, has been tremendously helped by some "insignificant" person, who never held a position of leadership in the church, who had no gifts that marked him out but who was always in his place, whose very face spoke of the love of the Lord, whose quiet prayer added power to the whole act of worship. Our churches are full of people like that. The man who thinks that he has no need to assemble with other believers in worship is saying, in effect, "I do not need the help of other people who can show in their living what a wonderful God we serve." We rob ourselves of opportunities of growth, and we do not contribute to the growth of others, when we fail to attend the service of worship. Worship in the believing community is so essential that it is true to assert that it is a major factor in the development of the Christian life.

PART
5

How Can I Grow Through Personal Evangelism?

PART

5

Is Personal Evangelism Important?

The Great Commission has never been withdrawn. The last commandment Jesus gave to his men before his ascension was, "Go, therefore, and make disciples of all nations, in Jerusalem, and in all Judea, and Samaria, and to the ends of the earth—baptizing them in the name of the Father and of the Son and of the Spirit." So long as there remain men and women who do not confess that "Jesus is the Christ come in the flesh" the church will have this command resting upon it.

It is thrilling to recall the urgency the disciples felt about telling the world about Jesus. They had seen what the forces of the Roman Empire and of Judaism could do when they came together in an unholy alliance, for they had seen their leader nailed to the cross. They were not impressed by the dominance of Imperial Rome as it bestrode the world from east to west. Every Roman soldier was a man and, therefore, reachable and in need of the gospel. Jews though they were, the first Christians were not overawed by the traditions of the Jewish fathers which, through nearly seven centuries, had already kept Judaism alive under Gentile skies. Every Jew was a man and could be reached by the "scandal" of the cross.

After weeks of patient waiting following his death the day of Pentecost comes and the power of the Holy Spirit is given. At once these recently bewildered disciples begin to explain clearly what the coming, the death, and the resurrection of Jesus mean to all men. Their message is summed up in Peter's words, "Let all the house of Israel know assuredly that God hath made him both Lord and Christ, this Jesus whom you crucified . . . Repent, and be baptized every one of you in the name of the Lord Jesus Christ for the forgiveness of sins" (Acts 2:36,38, RSV). A work had begun. Soon they were to be harassed and imprisoned and killed, but they were never to be silenced again. They would go on from strength to strength as they tried to tell all men everywhere about salvation through Christ.

How these men grew in the Lord as they reached out to win the lost in the power of the Spirit! Once, when Jesus was on the mount of transfiguration, they were unable to help a boy possessed by evil. Now they brought out their sick to Jerusalem from towns all around so that as Peter came by "at least his shadow might fall on some of them" (Acts 5:15, RSV). These were uneducated, common men but they spoke with an authority and such power of understanding that they reminded their hearers of that other one who had spoken with authority and "not as the scribes." Once they had to learn how to pray but now as they prayed prison doors flew open before them. Early one morning they had fled into the darkness as their Master was betrayed; now their courage sang songs in the night. Cowards they were, but as they spoke they grew in the Spirit's power until the whole world knew that something had happened.

The Great Commission of the worldwide proclamation of the gospel was made personal for Saul when he became Paul. "He is a chosen instrument of mine to carry my name before the Gentiles" (Acts 9:15, RSV). This was the man whose evangelical urgency was to drive him to the ends of the earth, enduring suffering and deprivation. As we think about his work for the Lord, phrase after compelling phrase tumble, one after the other, into the mind. "Woe is me if I preach not the Gospel! . . . I am become all things to all men that I might save some . . . I was determined to know nothing among you but Jesus and him crucified. . . . My heart's desire and longing for Israel is that they might be saved. . . . I

want to reap a harvest among you as well as the rest of the Gentiles.
. . . I wish you were as I am, but without these chains. . . . We
beseech you on behalf of Christ, be reconciled to God. . . . I feel
a divine jealousy for you, for I betrothed you to Christ. . . . Be
it far from me to glory except in the cross of our Lord Jesus Christ.
. . . To me was this grace given, to preach to the Gentiles the
unsearchable riches of Christ . . . until at the name of Jesus every
knee should bow and every tongue confess that Jesus Christ is Lord
to the glory of God the Father" (RSV).

That is an urgency every Christian needs to feel—an urgency
to tell others about the Lord Jesus Christ whose love and life are
beyond compare. Until this sense of urgency comes, it may be
asserted, the Christian has not claimed the glory of the fulness of
Christ for himself. The glory that he may have seen has not been
wonderful enough to put him under a compulsion to tell others.
He has not grown to see his responsibility. This responsibility
comes new upon the Lord's people in every generation. The world
can never be won for Jesus and remain that way. The glorious
challenge, "The world for Christ in this generation," which fired
so many students in the first decade of this century was authentic
and certainly inspired of God. But had they succeeded a universal
task would still have been left to us. Every new generation has to
be evangelized afresh because men die and men are born to take
their place. This fact alone is enough but today where one man
dies several are born to push their feet into his shoes. We drop
further and further behind as expanding populations race ahead
of us. The day of mission is now. And it will always be so. And
the Lord will always be calling, "Go, tell." Personal evangelism
is more than important; it is the divine imperative.

How Do I Grow?

Is Everybody an Evangelist?

But is this imperative incumbent upon everyone? The point can be made that the gifts of the Holy Spirit are many and varied and no one person has them all. They are given with a richness of power that can make little men able to move mountains but they are given with an economy that reminds the recipient of the seriousness of his task. A God-given gift is a precious possession to be used with the most dedicated stewardship. "His gifts were that some should be apostles, some prophets, some evangelists, some pastors and teachers" (Eph. 4:11, RSV). This text, which is one of several such references, clearly teaches that gifts are given selectively by the Holy Spirit, according to opportunity and need. Therefore not every one is called to be an evangelist.

This is obviously true and experience bears it out. Many men who are called to full-time, church-related vocations know well that their gifts are for the work of the ministry and not for the work of the itinerant evangelist, revival preacher. Not every one is a Billy Graham to whom the thousands flock and through whom the Spirit works in compelling power. Nor should every preacher try to be like Graham in his own small way. God has his specialists in every field of activity and he has some men in his church upon whom he has evidently placed his hand for the work of an evangelist. The majority obviously will not possess this gift.

But this does not absolve any Christian from the work of personal evangelism. Personal evangelism is the privilege and responsibility of every single Christian ever reached by his love. Personal evangelism is not preaching, nor arguing in philosophical terms, nor the discussion of theological dogmas. It is sharing the Lord Jesus Christ with someone who does not know him. It is telling another person of what Jesus has done and can do for them. It is loving a man, winning his trust, recognizing his need and bringing Jesus personally into the picture of his life. The task of reaching every man for Jesus is so overwhelmingly great and urgent that he passes none of his servants over in this job. Everyone who knows Jesus must tell others about him as persuasively as possible. The spoken testimony may not be very effective according to human standards and the man-to-man contact may be as far removed from the atmosphere of the great revival meeting as can be imagined but it is marvellous what the Lord can do with the faltering word sincerely spoken for him. Indeed it may be asserted that there are few people won in the powerful evangelistic crusade who have not previously been impressed by the living witness of some humble Christian.

We do not need to be experts either in theology or in evangelism techniques before we begin to speak up for him. If we really believe that we have found something good in Jesus, we shall tell others about him, just as we commend other good things that we experience to our friends. If we have a wonderful holiday in some vacation center and then hear an acquaintance saying that he is looking for a good place in which to spend a few days, we say to him, "Let us tell you about this place we recently visited." And then we describe the place, tell them how to get there, what it costs, what there is to do, whether it is suitable for children, and so on. We do not say to ourselves, "We would like to bring this lovely center to this person's attention but we are not trained travel agents so we will keep silent." We tell what we know. And that is often more satisfying and persuasive than the glossy brochure to which the travel agent turns for his secondhand information. When we practice personal evangelism, we tell people what we know, how we came to the experience, what we got from it, what it cost. As naturally and as simply as that the work of witnessing for Jesus, of winning people for him, begins. Anyone who has known his love can tell, must tell, of that experience.

The Joy of Winning Another

There is no joy known to the Christian that can be compared with that of winning another for Christ. The Christian life is the abundant life and when Jesus comes into man's life, man knows real joy. But the greatest of all the wonderful joys that follow is that which comes when God uses our witness to give another person a new hope and an assurance of abundant and everlasting life. This joy is one of those rich gifts that our God gives to encourage us to grow in knowledge and grace so that we may be more usable by him. "For what is our hope, or joy, or crown of rejoicing? Are not even ye in the presence of our Lord Jesus Christ at his coming?" (1 Thess. 2:19).

This joy is shared by others too. There is the person himself, who rejoices in his new salvation, who for the rest of his life (and through eternity!) will remember who it was that the Lord used to bring him to Jesus. There are others, members of our church, maybe, who come to hear of it and they rejoice too. Supremely, as the Scriptures say, "There is joy in heaven over one sinner who repents." "He shall see the fruit of the travail of his soul and be satisfied" (Isa. 53:11).

It is important to make the assertion that every Christian needs to ask himself whether he is prepared to lead a person right through the point of decision. Many ardent believers who faithfully witness to the Savior's love and power seem to have the idea that it is the pastor's job to help the inquirer through that last crucial step. Certainly this is a critical time in the prospective Christian's experience and care and wisdom need to be exercised to make sure that the final decision is made. But it remains true that many a decision for Christ has been missed because some ordinary Christian, having testified clearly in life and word to an inquirer, has held back at the crucial moment of decision and referred the person to a minister. The minister has been in the difficult position of having to gain the trust of the person quickly and of having to discover just where he stood in relation to the Lord. In the passing over of the reins, control has been lost. The decision which might have been made was not made because at the very point where continuity was essential there was an entirely unnecessary, and therefore artificial, break. In these days when so many are searching and so few find, it is essential that every believing Christian should be eager and prepared to take people right into the presence of Calvary. To stop a conversation short of decision may well mean that the decision will never be made.

The experience of winning men for Christ, of seeing men's lives being transformed by his loving friendship, keeps a man pressing forward in the Christian life. Only the best of our endeavor can be used for so high a purpose. Therefore we strive to offer our best and constantly to make that best better. Motivation of joy that is utterly unselfish, and still completely satisfying to the individual, keeps a man eager to learn more about the Lord whom he would commend to others. Many a missionary, many a minister, has been held to his task and calling for the sake of knowing this joy. It is a vital element in the development of the Christian life. "He that winneth souls is wise" (Prov. 11:30).

Preparation for Evangelism

Training in Techniques

Thousands of people have been won for Christ by people who have never had an hour of training in the techniques of evangelism. Any Christian who is really in love with the Lord Jesus will be an effective witness for him through the high quality of his life. The Holy Spirit, who is the only person who can convert, is perfectly able to move through the untrained, dedicated life. Yet it is certainly true to say that many more would have been won if Christians had learned how to use the gifts and opportunities that the Holy Spirit offers. When the Christian trains, he develops his latent powers and, additionally, makes himself better able to receive those extra powers which the Holy Spirit may wish to bestow.

The Christian will do well to attend any training which his church provides or that becomes available to him in his locality. Some interdenominational organizations, such as the Billy Graham Evangelistic Association and the Campus Crusades provide excellent training opportunities which give much help in the actual task of talking to an inquirer. However, training schemes provided by the denomination to which we belong are perhaps of greater value. They show not only how to counsel an inquirer but they deal with two other important aspects which may be linked with the nature of the church to which we belong. Different churches have different methods of reaching the unconverted and they have varied methods of welcoming converts into fellowship. If the personal evangelist is going to be as effective as he possibly can, he will need to be familiar with these things and will want to link his effort with the work of his church. If no training is arranged locally, it may be good to encourage a pastor or the leader of the church training program organization to plan such a course for the members. Leaders will usually give a ready response to such requests because they want to see their church reaching the lost and sometimes they need the encouragement of an ethusiastic Christian to set a training program in motion.

Individual study is also profitable. Church libraries and Christian book stores carry many books on this subject. The reader may turn to such books for discussions on the whole range of evangelism: what are the biblical bases, what techniques there are, how different types of people may be approached, how to understand the point of view of the inquirer, how to avoid pitfalls, how to make the gospel clear and persuasive, how to understand, and how to do a vast number of things.

Basic to all the study of methods is the most essential training of all, the study of the Bible as an aid to evangelism. Not only does it provide an incentive as it repeats, again and again, the message of the urgency of the task of evangelism but through its pages the witness learns to know God's plan of salvation. His mind becomes stored with passages and verses which he may use to commend not himself nor his own thinking but what God says. One of the most compelling aspects of Dr. Graham's preaching is his insistent emphasis on what the Bible says; this same emphasis is needed in the person-to-person conversation of one man trying to lead another to Christ. To sit alongside a person and, with an open Bible in hand, point out what God says is more effective than saying, "I have discovered . . ." The personal testimony is of tremendous importance but the witness is more effective when it is shown to be in line with what God has promised in his word. But that can only be done by the person who has made himself really familiar with the book. Our daily Bible study is important not for our own well-being alone but also that we may share the promises of God with others. The mind well stored with Bible knowledge will be able to draw out of the treasury things that will speak to the different needs and desires of other people. The Christian certainly has to grow continually in his knowledge of the Scriptures if the Spirit is to be able to use him in that way.

Spiritual training—Training in techniques is helpful; spiritual training is essential.

First, we will underline the truth that God can move most effectively through the fully consecrated life. When we begin to talk to a man about the Lord Jesus Christ, we have to recognize what we have noticed before, that the Spirit is the only one who can bring a person to the point of decision and that he is able to communicate more effectively with the spirit of a man than we can. Clear communication with other people in even the simplest things of life is often hard to achieve. We try to reach over the gulf that divides individual from individual only to lose the message half way. Even the most devoted couple celebrating their golden wedding will honestly say that there are depths of personality in each partner which the other has not plumbed nor understood. If this is true of the relationship between people who know each other as they talk about common concerns, how much more true will it be of that conversation which has, as its aim, decision for Christ. In it we are sharing information and experience at such a deep level that it is hard to find words adequate to communicate the message. But, in addition, we are also trying to effect a change in a man's attitudes in the most fundamental way. We are trying to change his relationship to God and that will change every other relationship in his life to a smaller or greater degree. Old habits will have to be changed; a new evaluation of material possessions and the way of getting and using them will come. Many friends will have to be left behind and new demands upon time and energy will be made. A new center for life will challenge everything that goes on in its radius. Such a change can only come through the direct intervention of the Holy Spirit. He is the only one who can reach over the barriers of understanding and break down resistance to another man's ideas. This is what the Bible means when it says that no man can say that Jesus is Lord except by the Holy Spirit (1 Cor. 12:3; 1 John 4:2). This activity at the point of decision is the completion of a work begun by the Holy Spirit. Biblical belief is that the Spirit is always seeking for the lost and that the very situation in which the work of personal evangelism is to be done is of his creating. The work of conversion in its initiation, persuasion, and conviction is God's, working through the Holy Spirit. The responsibility for the act of conversion is his alone; our responsibility is to be available to serve as his agent.

We can never know when he may want to use us. Therefore, it is essential that the Christian should keep his life close to the Lord so that at any time the power of the Spirit may flow unhindered through his life. To be more specific he will, by his constant prayer and Bible study, make his spiritual sensitivity and alertness such that he will be able to respond readily to the Spirit's leading. He will be eager for that leading. A mind that is trained to receive, through daily prayer and Bible reading, that message which the Holy Spirit would give will be better able to be directed by him in critical moments of a conversation with a seeker. For example, the Spirit can only bring to remembrance the words of the Scriptures in the mind of a person whose deliberate study has stored his mind with the Scriptures and has given him a knowledge about where he can find what he needs. All this actually can happen to an ordinary person and when it does a mighty confidence in the personal activity of God fills his life.

When the Spirit is active, there is a real communication. As we talk, we know that we are reaching, rather the *Holy Spirit is reaching,* the heart of the other person. Often there is a feeling of the personal presence of the Spirit so real as to defy description. We know that he is really at work in the mind and heart of the inquirer and that if we simply follow him we shall have the privilege of seeing a man being born again. What God can do through the consecrated life is beyond belief. Heart, mind, and will committed to him become instruments in the hand of a mighty God who changes men. Christians who have what our fathers loved to call "a burden for souls" will grow because they will see their need to be constantly ready to be used by their Lord. Prayer, Bible study, worship, obedience to his call, will all be drawn into play so that the witness may always be ready to reach a man for salvation in Christ, not in his own wisdom but in that which the Spirit supplies.

What Do I Say?

It follows from this emphasis on the Holy Spirit's work in conversion that there is no magic formula which can be given to the would-be evangelist that will get results every time. This is a place where some books and training programs on personal evangelism oversimplify the work. No two men are alike in their needs, experiences, or opportunities and therefore no one pattern of conversation will fit every case. For the same reasons no one set of proof texts will fit every case. Men are not machines and the soul-winning conversation cannot be computerized. Sometimes a man may be won by a single conversation but this is rare and it is more usual that he will be won after much patient witness in visitation and prayer and talk.

Yet it remains true that there are some things that can be stated in general terms which need only little interpretation by the witness. These things are set out, for example, in printed materials made available to personal evangelists in the Campus Crusade, the Billy Graham Crusades, and in the Southern Baptists' WIN (Witness Involvement Now) materials. These include tracts for the inquirer and help for the witness as he makes his contact, witnesses, and then testifies.

Most of these materials develop the three basic facts of the "plan of salvation." We will state these propositions in non-theological, non-biblical language because a majority of persons with whom we may talk about steps leading to faith in Christ will have little understanding of "church" terminology. There are three propositions that may form the basis of the conversation which leads to decision.

Every man has some need.

Jesus can meet every man's need.

His help has to be accepted.

Many writers would prefer to phrase these propositions in the following way.

Every man is a sinner.

Jesus died to save all men from sin.

Man's repentance is followed by forgiveness.

The presentation of an alternate wording for these phrases does not imply any disagreement with them. They are definitely true to the Scriptures and will certainly be needed at some point of climax in the inquirer's life. The alternative series of propositions in terms of "need" rather than of "sin" is suggested because in an amoral society like ours the word "sin" is not understood by many of the "lost" persons whom we would help. For them "sin" is a quaint Victorian hangover. At best their concept of sin is doing lots of little bad things that they hope may never be found out but are of little consequence either way. It is a language that does not relate to them. Moreover, these inadequate ideas are sometimes held by those who would witness. Our aim is to restore biblical thinking about sin. Christians have rightly learned to think of sin as an internal wrong attitude rather than an external breaking of some moral law. Sin is despair as well as adultery. Therefore we use the word "need" to avoid the danger of seeing sin as being only the breaking of moral precepts, which would be the way in which a non-Christian westerner would undoubtedly interpret it today. This is an inadequate interpretation and leaves many amoral, unconverted people with the impression that Christianity is not relevant to their needs. But the *needs* of the unreached man are the result of sin, using that word in its fullest meaning. Sin is that wrong relationship with God which results in that frustration, hopelessness, purposelessness, which tries to find release through immorality of one form or another. To be "lost" is not so much to be condemned as to be utterly lonely, without any motive or meaning in life, because one is separated from God. The lost sheep was not "lost" because it was in rebellion against the shepherd but because it had strayed into the wilderness. This is what the Scriptures teach and that is what contemporary man needs to hear. Jesus and his cross deal with every need resulting from man's estrangement from God, not only with that immorality which is usually only a symptom of a deeper disease in the heart.

Therefore as we seek to witness to people for Jesus we need to do what he did and speak to their real needs. Sometimes Jesus did link his merciful work with the forgiveness of sin and clearly said so because in those cases cleansing from the power and guilt of sin was the dominant need. However, on many an occasion he dealt with the apparent need first. He did not make everybody fit into a plan of salvation but he interpreted the plan to meet individual needs. He did not require repentance from Zacchaeus before he would have anything to do with him. He called to a lonely, ostracized little man, "Zacchaeus, make haste and come down; for I must stay at your house today" (Luke 19:5, RSV). Jesus met the need that was uppermost in Zacchaeus' heart, his need for fellowship, and then followed a wonderful moral transformation. In the story of the rich man who came asking, "What must I do to have eternal life?" Jesus surveyed the Ten Commandments, heard the man say, "All these I have kept," and then pointed out that the man had a need beyond the moral law—he needed to be set free from his dependance on material things. Jesus did not deny the man's protest that he was morally good; he tried to make him face up to his complacency about spiritual values (Matt. 19:20). Luke tells us that when Jesus and his disciples were walking to Jerusalem he would stop and invite people to follow him. One did not follow because he could not give up his creature comforts, another because of the laudable desire to go and bury his dead father, another because he wanted to take some time for the innocent pursuit of trying out a new possession, a team of oxen. Yet another made the bland statement, "I have married a wife. Therefore I cannot come." These statements may be dismissed as excuses and the argument from silence may be offered that what kept them from following Jesus was their sin. If "sin" is seen as separation from God, then that interpretation is in accord with the Lord's evident attitude to them. But the story does not say that immoral acts, the breaking of moral precepts, prevented them from following; their sin was found in their wrong sets of values and attitudes to life, their basic separation from God.

It is this basic problem (or need) which the witness faces whenever he begins the task of leading a man out of darkness into the light of the gospel. This is why it is recommended that we should try to see the fundamental need rather than the expression of it in the immoral act. This is not always easy for the Christian, who may be easily shocked by what he regards as immoral behavior so that he cannot see the crying need of the soul out of tune with its maker. We see the long hair and the dirt of the hippie and dismiss his cry for love as a deliberate distortion of the fundamental Christian word. We tend to despise the drug addict (or the alcohol addict) and fail to see their longing to know what it is all about. We are hurt by the indifference of our neighbors to our churches and we therefore overlook their disillusionment and despair.

The ability to understand men better than themselves is an insight which only the Lord has. But the Lord's people have been assigned the task of being ambassadors to people in the lost world, "as though God did beseech you through me," as Paul put it. Really thrilling growth will come in the Christian's own life if he will see that he has to love God so much that the Holy Spirit can communicate with and through him, that he has to love all men so much that he may have a Christ-like, Spirit-inspired understanding of his contemporaries' fundamental needs. To meet that need the witness must learn more and more about the problems of men and what they mean. He will know well that he himself will need to keep so close to the Lord that he will love even with the love of Christ. When we have come to that place where we see what "lostness" or "sin" really means, we shall be much more effective in showing how any man can find his need met in the love of the Lord Jesus Christ. Like the people we see in the New Testament, transformation of the moral life will follow but first of all we have to be "all things to all men," "to sit where they sit," to love as Jesus loved.

When we have recognized the underlying need of the first proposition, we can move forward to the second proposition, that Jesus can meet the need whatever it may be. Sometimes it will be the superficial need of the lonely man (like Zacchaeus), sometimes it will be gross immorality (like the woman at the well), sometimes it will be at a time of bereavement (like Martha's), sometimes it will be a soul-consuming spiritual need (like Saul's on the Damascus road), sometimes it will be when the heart is ready to face the issues of life and death (like Nicodemus). When the need is recognized then comes the persuasive assurance that the Lord Jesus is able to deal with every need. Few people will refuse to listen when someone who loves Jesus tries to show how the love of the Savior answers every man's need. At this point the witness' own devotion and commitment to the Lord may be that which the Spirit may use to bring conviction.

Next comes the third proposition, the personal acceptance of the help Jesus gives. "Trust Jesus to do for you now what you need now. Begin to trust him just where you are now. Believe that what he did for the men and women whose stories are in the Bible he will do for you today. Take his promise and believe." Wherever possible the person coming to decision should be encouraged to put that decision into words. A thought expressed in words is a thought clarified. A decision verbalized is a decision crystalized. The fact that another has heard the confession of faith commits the new believer more fully to the decision he has made.

Two Pitfalls to Avoid

These comments will have shown that our aim in evangelism is not that of commending our local church but that of commending Jesus as the answer to man's need. This does not imply that commendation of the local church is out of place in the word of the witness. The church is the body of Christ. It provides the atmosphere in which both the young and the mature Christian may grow in Christ. It is the place where Christians join together to meet their responsibilities. It is good to be able to speak highly of the pastor and the people or even to show how our denomination is trying to serve people in the name of the Lord. Yet in spite of this the witness must guard against giving the impression that his concern for the person with whom he is talking arises from the desire to see his church flourish as a society (or even as a club). This may be far from his thought but the unbeliever frequently has the attitude of mind which questions motives, "Why should he be concerned about me? What's in it for him? Must be that he wants to see the Baptists beating the Methodists!" When we commend Jesus and Jesus only, this is avoided.

Commending him also leads to an emphasis on the priority of allegiance to Christ before allegiance to the local church. Very very few people believe that salvation is a free gift; they persistently believe that they must do something to earn it. Church service is therefore seen as the means of salvation. And most people do not like what they see in the modern church. Others substitute their activity of church works for the more costly committal of the whole life to the Lord. If we commend the church to the inquirer, he may substitute the shadow for the substance, church activity for transforming faith in Jesus. Our message must be Christ; Christ's church is of vital importance but it is secondary to him.

The second major pitfall that we need to avoid in the witnessing conversation is argument. Argument is a very different thing than discussion. In discussion two minds that are are not opposed to each other share their differing ideas in an attempt to broaden knowledge and thinking. In argument two minds which are opposed to each other seek to conquer the opponent's point of view with one-sided statements of position. A common mark of argument is the closed mind and the failure to appreciate the opponent's position. Often it arouses deep emotions which may be tied in with prejudices. In witnessing it is easy for discussion to become argument. This happens quickly if the witness is too dogmatic or fails clearly to show a readiness to understand the outlook and problems of the person to whom he speaks. If he backs his contact into a corner by his argument his contact is likely to fight back in defense. It is this fighting back that just has to be avoided because it means disaster in the witnessing conversation. In order to fight back the contact will think up all the reasons why he should not become a Christian. As he introduces these reasons into argument they become his own. He may be forced into a position of direct opposition to Christ that he never held before. Uncertainties about the Christian life can be turned into definite opposition. This is obviously the worst thing that can happen as a result of our witness. Argument has driven the man away from Christ.

But how can the witness, in presenting his message with conviction, stay out of argument? First, genuine respect and concern for the person as a person (rather than as a prospect) must be clearly evident in his total attitude. This concern and respect for the individual will make the witness eager to cooperate with rather than score over his contact. Second, he must seek to talk *with,* not *to* or *against,* his friend. Third, he should not attack the ideas advanced by the person but should simply commend Jesus. As soon as any sign is seen that an argument is developing, the witness should bring the talk to an end graciously and leave with the comment that he will eagerly anticipate another conversation in the near future. When that opportunity comes he will be able to lead the conversation again along constructive lines.

Dealing with Problems in the Witness

Overcoming timidity and uncertainty.—Witnessing to people about the Lord Jesus Christ does require a lot of courage. The Christian faith touches a man at the innermost part of his life and anyone who would reach in there has to be certain of what he is doing. Because the gospel's effect is so important and intimate we are often reluctant to take the risk and talk about things that really matter. It is easier to discuss the weather, or last night's ball game, or the stock market, or some new book, or the pastor! But most of these things are superficial and they obviously do not meet a person's deepest hungers. To do that we have to grow in our own commitment to Christ as we overcome timidity and reluctance.

Timidity should be seen, firstly, as a genuine spiritual response to the Lord's call. Some of the greatest figures of the Bible seemed to look over their shoulders when God called them to service, as though he could not possibly be speaking to them but must be addressing someone behind them. Moses says, "Who am I, that I should go to Pharaoh?" (Ex. 3:11, RSV). Isaiah, overawed by his vision, pleads, "Woe is me! For I am undone; . . . I dwell in the midst of a people of unclean lips" (Isa. 6:5). Jeremiah's protest is, "Ah, Lord God! behold, I cannot speak: for I am but a child" (Jer. 1:6). When Ezekiel described his call he says that he fell on his face when he saw the glory of the Lord because of his feelings of humility and insufficiency. Jonah was so reluctant that he actually went in a direction opposite to that which the Lord wanted him to take. Even Paul found it necessary to go into the wilderness for twelve years before he started his missionary work.

These facts may be somewhat negative but it is an encouragement to learn from the Scriptures that the Lord can take the reluctant and use them effectively in his service. In fact, it could be asserted that unless a man is aware of his own insufficiency he is not usable by the Lord; he is not sensitive enough either to the magnitude of the God who calls or to the magnitude of what he might do to another person's life. But in facing uncertainty and timidity the witness may grow in his dependence upon God and in his understanding of the Lord's will.

A helpful thought in the process of overcoming the initial reluctance is to analyze, honestly and deliberately, our own varied experience of the Lord's love and to see in those experiences the genuine experience of a twentieth-century man. No man has precisely the same needs as another; but one man's needs are every man's needs. Men are so much alike that the psychologist can generalize about his needs and reactions. Though we are all so amazingly different it is the difference of the arrangement of the same basic constituents. All the music in the world, from the established classic to the most ephemeral pop song, is made up of the same basic scale of eight notes. "There, but for the grace of God, go I" is a reminder of the fact that the same basics are in every man's life but they are arranged and played upon differently. This means that my experience of life is a basic human experience of life. What the Lord does for me he can do for the murderer *(there go I in other circumstances . . .),* or the college professor *(. . . if I had had his opportunities),* or the hippie *(but I've got the peace, the love, the real thing),* or the lonely, the bereaved, the shy, the depressed *(What a friend I have in Jesus . . .).* There is no such thing as the entirely unique man. All men are needy men. The idol has feet of clay and the insignificant holds a world of potentialities within himself. When we speak of the twentieth-century man we speak as twentieth-century men, subject to the same stresses, pressures, temptations, and disillusionments as any other person who shares the same atmosphere with us. Speak of need and we speak to the world. "We speak that we know and testify that which we have seen." Therefore we need not be silent because we are not sure that what we have to say is important. If it is really important to us it will be so to other men.

Linked closely to this problem is our own lack of knowledge. Stress has already been laid upon a need for Bible study that will enable the witness to give an account of the faith that is in him. The more knowledge we have of his word the more confident we shall be. At this point we would stress the fact that the Christian must not wait until "he knows it all" before he begins to testify. Such a standard would muzzle the mouth permanently. If, in the course of witnessing, questions are raised to which the witness does not know the answer he should honestly tell his contact that he does not know. He may suggest that *both* of them should try to discover the answer that the Bible (or "the Christian faith" with one who is suspicious of the Bible) might give.

A timid person seeking to be obedient to the Lord's will should never forget that his work is preceded by the work of the Holy Spirit, done in the power of the Holy Spirit, and is sustained by the grace of that same Spirit. The Spirit of the Lord can work behind locked doors. The needs of man are all known to God and he can send the right person to be his agent in answering them. Jesus promised that his Spirit would give us words to say, that the Spirit would bring to our remembrance the things he said and would lead us into all truth. It is really helpful to claim these promises definitely and precisely before witnessing. See every meeting, whether it be the planned appointment or the chance meeting, as something that God has had a hand in planning and the witness will have a greater confidence that the Spirit will use him in that situation. Every person who seeks to commend Christ to others needs to be aware that the Spirit of God is working both through him and in the other person.

Secular educationalists write of the "teachable moment," a moment which comes in the pupil's thinking when he is all prepared as a result of his study, thinking, research, and experience to accept the new idea. For the teacher this is the moment pregnant with opportunity. In the work of the Christian this "teachable moment" comes not only because of study and reasoning but because the Spirit can work personally in any man's life to bring about that "teachable moment" when the new truth may be received. This will be the moment of rebirth, when a man is "born of God" (1 John 4:7). The reluctant servants of the Bible times became great because they believed in the help that their God would give. To Moses God said, "Certainly I will be with thee." Isaiah saw the seraphim and heard one say, "This hath touched thy lips, and thine iniquity is taken away." Promises were given to Jeremiah, "Say not, I am a child . . . I am with thee . . . I have put words within thy mouth." Grovelling Ezekiel heard a voice, "Stand upon thy feet" and he wrote, "The Spirit entered into me when he spake unto me, and set me on my feet, that I heard him that spake unto me." This is the way in which God will work today when the timid man offers himself as a witness. And it is certainly a growing experience.

Like so many experiences of the Christian life the knowledge of God's strengthening and guiding comes only in the practice of the witness. And that is a real part of the problem for the timid believer. How can he begin? Just getting started is the main problem. Two suggestions can be made. It is a tremendous help if a would-be witness can begin his service in the normal program of his church. Many churches learn of people who are unsaved and unchurched through censuses, prospect searches and ordinary neighborhood contacts. Information about the prospect's life and background are usually available. These people are visited by assignment made through the appropriate church organization, usually the Sunday School. The new witness can be invited to accompany an experienced visitor on early visits to the prospect and thus be helped in the early stages of his work. (It is usually advisable for the experienced visitor to witness alone when the conversations with the prospect indicate that he is nearing a decision.) The person making the assignment for the two-by-two visit (which is scriptural) will bear in mind the special "in-service training" aspect of the visit and will not assign the new worker to a case which is obviously unusual or full of difficulties. Thus the beginning is made and a joyful experience of use by the Lord is begun.

The second suggestion concerns the spiritual preparation of the new witness. He should make the fullest preparation he can, along lines suggested in this chapter, and should then, through prayer, make a definite offer of his service to the Lord. His constant prayer on this matter will be matched by an alert watching for the moment of opportunity. When this moment comes the witness sees that this is God already working with him. He is not opening the door; it is being opened. And the God who opens the door will be the God who will enter it with the witness. He never calls without equipping. So the new witness begins his work with an experience of the Father's interest and cooperation and goes on in that knowledge to deeper experiences of his sustaining grace.

Overcoming Censoriousness

At the other end of the spectrum of Christian witness is censoriousness, a failing which makes the witness useless in his work. His attitude implies superiority and condescension. It implies judgment and condemnation of the life of the person to whom he would talk. It may suggest that any person who rejects or disagrees with his pronouncements is a fool. And this is one of the perils of the Christian walk which is most difficult to avoid. But if any testifying is to be effective it is a danger that has to be recognized and overcome.

The most important step in overcoming censoriousness is an honest recognition and acknowledgement of the failing in the life of the witness. Once he recognizes that he is censorious he is well on the way to recovery. The problem is an attitude of mind and heart and honest thinking about the witness' spiritual status and motivation in evangelism will contribute to the eradication of the fault.

When we have been disciples of Jesus for a long time, we tend to forget the sense of wonder that he should die to commend his love to us. Pride in our salvation becomes pride in ourselves as Christians. We forget how low we were; we are only conscious of how high we have reached. Hence we commend ourselves and not

Jesus. Therefore we need to get back to the sense of utter unworthiness which would make us praise him in Wesley's words of wonder,

> And can it be that I should gain
> An interest in the Savior's blood?
> Died he for me who caused his pain,
> For me—who him to death pursued?
>> Amazing grace, how can it be
>> That thou, my God, shoulds't die for me?

There is nothing in ourselves that we can boast about but we can boast about him with happiness and confidence. If we put the stress on what we have done, how *we* found him, how *we* wisely turned from an (exaggeratedly) evil life, how *we* have served faithfully, how *we* want to see others becoming like us, people will turn away from our self-pride and will not see the Savior. But if we marvel at what he has done, how *he* found us, how *he* helps us with our problems when we let him down, how *he* will never let us down, how he is eager to do the same for everyone then our testimony will be more readily accepted. There has to be less of self and more of him.

There is also a need to reconsider our motivation in evangelism. Why do we seek men for Christ? In order to have a victory notched up to our credit? Or to add another member to boost the statistical record of our Sunday School? Or to experience the common human satisfaction of influencing the life of another person? These are common motives and all of them may lead to a censorious or condescending attitude of mind. There is only one reason why we should seek the lost and that is because the Lord Jesus Christ loved them and died for them. It is not enough to make our love for the lost the motive of evangelism, for that is too self-centered. If our personal "love" is the motivating factor, we remain the dominant figure in the work of redemption being offered to the inquirer. Our love, moreover, can tire and fail and our testimony therefore cease. But his love does not change. It is that never-ending love which will enable us to go on and on, loving simply and sincerely people who are unlovely. A "passion for souls" needs to be the outcome of our love for the Savior. When we love him, we love our fellow men. When we love him so deeply that his love shines through all the distortion and the dust of our lives, then others will respond.

When we love God with all our heart, then people will know that we love them for themselves and not for what we hope to get out of them. Genuine love for Christ finds expression in our love for our fellows that they will recognize. They seldom mistake genuine concern for condescension or superiority. Such love is free from judgement and condemnation though it leads the person who becomes aware of its presence to judge himself.

A spirit of self-satisfaction and of self-achievement in the Christian walk kills growth. As Jesus said, those who make an arrogant display of spirituality already have their reward, but it is the humble man whose only pride is in his Lord who will be filled by the love of God, the grace of the Lord Jesus Christ, and the power of the Holy Spirit. Just as it is true to say that many churches are dying because they never see conversions in their services so is it true to say that the faith of many Christians grows weak because they have not seen the Lord working through them. In a world of men and women who need some answers to fundamental questions about the meaning and purpose of life the Christian must share the insights that God has given to him. When he does that he realizes afresh the wonder of the Savior's sufficiency, meeting man's every need, including his own. He who shares Christ grows in Christ.

PART
6
An Encouragement

CONCLUSION:

6

An Encouragement

The apostle Paul discusses with the Corinthians the theme of what Christians mean to God (2 Cor. 2:14 to 3:6). He glories in the fact that Christ leads his followers in a triumphant pageant, because they are to share in his conquest of sin and death. As they follow him, they will be reminders to the Father of the Son. But Paul does not put it in that mundane way; he uses colorful poetic language which paints a richer picture of what the believer may mean to God. He assures the reader that the believer will spread the fragrance of Christ everywhere and be to God the aroma of Christ. The very sweetness and beauty of Jesus will be reflected in him. We may catch the vision of Paul and use biblical images that Christians have loved to apply to Jesus, who has seemed to them to be the Fairest of Ten Thousand, the Lily of the Valley, the Rose of Sharon, the altogether lovely, the Brightest Morning Star, the effulgence of His glory, the Lamb of God without blemish and say, "That is the person whom we bring to God's mind!"

> Let the beauty of Jesus be seen in me,
> All his wondrous compassion and purity!

That is what this book is all about in the final analysis. Growing in the Christian religion means nothing if it does not mean growing in Christ, becoming more like him "until we all attain to the unity of the faith and of the knowledge of the Son of God, to mature manhood, to the measure of the stature of the fulness of Christ"

(Eph. 4:13, RSV). This is an impossibly high standard to strive for, let alone maintain. With Paul we find a compulsion to say, "Who is sufficient for these things?" (2 Cor. 2:16, RSV). There are so many things required of the Christian that it is easy to conclude that the standards are so far beyond our reach that it is vain even to attempt to touch them. Personal purity in thought, word, and deed is difficult to achieve in itself but that is only a beginning. We have seen that the Christian cannot live in isolation and that there are exceedingly high principles to be followed in relationships with other people in all the different areas of our living. Loving the lovely is hard enough sometimes; but who can constantly be obedient to the precept, "Love your enemies and those that harm you"? And yet the heights of behavior are not fully surveyed! It is the Christian's responsibility so to live that men will see in him the likeness of the Lord Jesus. There are standards for his spiritual life in relationship with his God. He expects one day to stand before that God to whom all is known, even the secret desires of the heart. Who, indeed, is sufficient for these things? Such things are impossible and it may be that some have come to the end of this book with such an overwhelming sense of their inadequacy that they feel that this Christian walk is not for them. To them we would address this word of encouragement. God, through his grace and love, is alongside us in everything that we do.

There is that other side of the picture. With every assertion of a standard set we have seen that the Lord will provide the specific help, from his infinite resources, for all our needs. Indeed many of the standards have been described because the purpose for the provision of a gift or power could only be understood by looking at the situation in which the gift could be used. Again and again we marvel in the astonishing richness of what God has provided for us: he starts the work in our conversion, he awakens our conscience, he sets the challenging ideal, he guides us to the things we should do, he gives us the power to do them, he comes down into our daily experience, he provides lines of communication, he fills our souls with awe at his presence, he assures us of his continuing love when we fail, he allows us freedom to attempt or not to attempt, he picks us up when we are down, he chooses to speak through us to other people, he gives us words to say, he gives us courage to endure pain, to remain humble in success . . . he forgives us when we turn away from him . . . and when the whole catalog of his goodness is complete (can it ever be?) he then takes us to live with him for ever.

The apostle asks the question, "Who is sufficient for these things?" and we all say, "That's how we feel!" But then he answers his own question, "Our sufficiency is from God" (2 Cor. 3:5, RSV). This was where his great confidence lay. It was not in himself. He, like us, was unable to do anything of real value by himself. But in those days following his Damascus road experience he learned that the distinctive difference between the old way of Judaism and the new life of the Way lay precisely at this point. The old religion said, "This is what a holy God expects you to do." Saul the Jew failed to do it though he had high courage and strong resolution. In the Christian faith Paul heard the message, "This is what a holy God expects you to do and in Christ he provides the means to do it." In Jesus the converted Jew found the help he needed, "I can do all things through Christ that strengtheneth me!" Jesus still lived. That meant eternal newness of life.

Today the path of the Christian is as difficult as it has ever been. So many voices, some sweet and enticing, some hard and demanding, some subtle and self destroying, call from the world for his attention and divert his concentration from the Way of Life. Such conditions call not for a reduced standard of Christian living but for a triumphant declaration that this is the only way to satisfaction, peace, joy, meaning, experience, abundant life. Alone we fail. But our sufficiency too is of God. Through him we can attain the impossible and become, through his strength, greater people than we ever thought possible. If we give him a real opportunity of working through us and in us he will assuredly do so. Jesus still lives. He can live in you, if you give him the opportunity.

> O thou Spirit divine,
> All my nature refine,
> Till the beauty of Jesus is seen in me.

Broadman Books for Further Reading

MURRAY, RALPH L. *The Biblical Shape of Hope.* Nashville: Broadman Press, 1971.

ROARK, DALLAS M. *The Christian Faith: An Introduction to Christian Thought.* Nashville: Broadman Press, 1969.

SCARBOROUGH, L. R. *With Christ After the Lost* (Revised by E. D. Head). Nashville: Broadman Press, 1953.

TRESCH, JOHN W. *A Prayer for All Seasons.* Nashville: Broadman Press, 1971.

WARD, WAYNE E., and GREEN, JOSEPH F., editors. *Is the Bible a Human Book?* Nashville: Broadman Press, 1970.